THE SECRET HISTORY OF
FREEMASONRY

THE SECRET HISTORY OF
FREEMASONRY

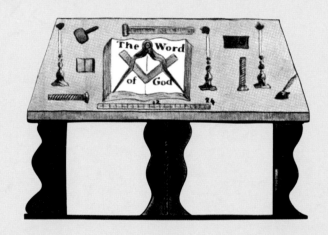

A complete illustrated reference to the
Brotherhood of Masons, covering 1000 years
of ritual and rites, signs and symbols, from
ancient foundation to the modern day

JEREMY HARWOOD

LORENZ BOOKS

This edition is published by Lorenz Books

Lorenz Books is an imprint of
Anness Publishing Ltd
Hermes House, 88–89 Blackfriars Road
London SE1 8HA
tel. 020 7401 2077; fax 020 7633 9499
www.lorenzbooks.com; info@anness.com

© Anness Publishing Ltd 2006

UK agent: The Manning Partnership Ltd
6 The Old Dairy, Melcombe Road
Bath BA2 3LR
tel. 01225 478 444; fax 01225 478 440
sales@manning-partnership.co.uk

UK distributor: Grantham Book Services Ltd
Isaac Newton Way, Alma Park
Industrial Estate
Grantham, Lincs NG31 9SD
tel. 01476 541080; fax 01476 541061
orders@gbs.tbs-ltd.co.uk

North American agent/distributor:
National Book Network
4501 Forbes Boulevard, Suite 200
Lanham, MD 20706
tel. 301 459 3366; fax 301 429 5746
www.nbnbooks.com

Australian agent/distributor: Pan Macmillan Australia
Level 18, St Martins Tower
31 Market St, Sydney, NSW 2000
tel. 1300 135 113; fax 1300 135 103
customer.service@macmillan.com.au

New Zealand agent/distributor: David Bateman Ltd
30 Tarndale Grove, Off Bush Road
Albany, Auckland
tel. (09) 415 7664; fax (09) 415 8892

Designed and produced for Anness Publishing by
THE BRIDGEWATER BOOK COMPANY LTD.

Publisher Joanna Lorenz
Editorial Director Helen Sudell
Editor Sarah Doughty
Designer Barbara Zuñiga
Art Director Michael Whitehead
Editorial Readers Rosanna Fairhead, Jay Thundercliffe
Production Controller Wendy Lawson

10 9 8 7 6 5 4 3 2 1

PICTURE ACKNOWLEGEMENTS

Anness Publishing would like to thank the following for kindly supplying
photographs for this book: 1 Fidelity Masonic Supplies: 2 Grand British Lodge
of Columbia: 3 The Stapleton Collection (STC): 4 l STC, c STC: 5 t STC,
br STC, bl STC: 6–7 tl, r STC: 8 tl STC, bl Bridgeman Art Library (BAL):
9 tl STC, tr Grand British Lodge of Columbia: 10 tl BAL, b STC: 11 tl STC,
tr BAL: 12–13 tl, r STC: 13 STC: 14 tl STC, c STC, bl STC: 15 tr Tim
Wallace-Murphy, tl Tim Wallace-Murphy, br STC: 16 tl BAL, bl BAL: 17 tL
STC, tr STC, br STC: 18 tl STC, tr Grand British Lodge of Columbia, bl BAL:
19 tr STC, br STC: 20 tl STC, br STC, bl STC: 21 tl STC, tr STC, c Coral
Mula, br STC: 22 tl STC, bl STC: 23 tl STC, tr, STC, bl STC: 24 tl STC,
b STC: 25 t STC, tr STC, bl STC: 26 tl BAL, b STC: 27 t BAL, br STC: 28 tl
STC, br STC, l Grand British Lodge of Columbia: 29 t Grand British Lodge of
Columbia, tr STC, b STC: 30 tl BAL, b BAL: 31 tL STC, tr STC, br STC:
32–3 tl, r BAL: 34 tl STC, br STC, bl STC: 35 tl STC, tr © 2005
JupiterImages Corporation: 36 tl STC, b STC: 37 tl STC, br STC: 38 tl STC,
bl STC: 39 t STC, br STC, b STC: 40 tl STC, br STC, l STC: 41 tl STC, tr
STC, br STC: 42 tl STC, b Library and Museum of Freemasonry: 43 tl STC,
r STC, br BAL: 44 tl STC, b BAL: 45 tr BAL, br Grand British Lodge of
Columbia: 46 tl STC, bl STC: 47 t STC, br STC: 48–49 tl, r BAL: 50 tl STC,
c STC, lc STC: 51 r STC, bl STC, bl STC: 52 t STC, b STC: 53 tr STC, b
STC: 54 tl STC, b STC: 55 tl STC, br STC: 56 tl STC, l STC: 57 t Fidelity
Masonic Supplies, b STC: 58 tl Grand British Lodge of Columbia, bl Grand
British Lodge of Columbia: 59 tr STC, br STC: 60 tl STC, cr STC, cl STC,
br Grand British Lodge of Columbia, bl STC: 61 t STC, br STC: 62 Grand
British Lodge of Columbia, cr STC, cl STC: 63 t STC, br Grand British Lodge
of Columbia: 64 tl STC, cl STC, b STC: 65 t STC: 66 Fidelity Masonic
Supplies, bl STC: 67 tl STC, tr Fidelity Masonic Supplies: 68 tl Fidelity
Masonic Supplies, c STC, bl Fidelity Masonic Supplies: 69 tr STC, br Grand
British Lodge of Columbia, bl STC: 70 tl Fidelity Masonic Supplies, r STC,
l Grand British Lodge of Columbia: 71 tl STC, r Fidelity Masonic Supplies:
72 tl BAL, bl Library and Museum of Freemasonry: 73 t STC, r STC, b BAL:
74 tl Grand British Lodge of Columbia, b Grand British Lodge of Columbia:
75 c Grand British Lodge of Columbia, r STC: 76 tl STC, b STC: 77 tr STC:
78 tl BAL, b Grand British Lodge of Columbia: 79 BAL: 80 tl Grand British
Lodge of Columbia, bl Grand British Lodge of Columbia: 81 tl STC, r Grand
British Lodge of Columbia: 82 tl STC, c Grand British Lodge of Columbia,
bc STC, bl STC: 83 t STC, cr Coral Mula, b STC: 84 tl STC, br STC, bc STC,
bl STC: 85 t Grand British Lodge of Columbia, br STC, bc STC, bl STC: 86 tl
STC, c STC: 87 tl Coral Mula, tr STC, br STC: 88 tl BAL, bl BAL: 89 tr BAL,
br Grand British Lodge of Columbia, bl Grand British Lodge of Columbia:
90 tl Fidelity Masonic Supplies, bl Grand British Lodge of Columbia: 91 tl
Fidelity Masonic Supplies, c Fidelity Masonic Supplies, r Fidelity Masonic
Supplies, bl STC: 92 tr STC, Grand British Lodge of Columbia, bl STC: 93 tr
STC, br STC, bl Tim Wallace-Murphy: 94 c STC, bl STC: 95 tl STC, c STC,
br STC: 96 tr STC, c STC, bl STC: Front flap top The Stapleton Collection
(STC), centre Grand British Lodge of Columbia, front cover and back cover left
to right top, The Stapleton Collection (STC), below Fidelity Masonic Supplies,
back flap top STC.

Every effort has been made to obtain permission to reproduce copyright
material, but there may be cases where we have been unable to trace a copyright
holder. The publisher will be happy to correct any omissions in future printings.

Images are listed in clockwise order from the top (t = top, c = centre,
b = bottom, r = right, l = left, tr = top right etc.)

CONTENTS

Part One

INTRODUCING FREEMASONRY — 6

Ideas and Ideals — 8
Origins and Allegories — 10

Part Two

LEGEND AND HISTORY — 12

The Knights Templar — 14
Legend and Ritual — 16
The Hiramic Legend — 18
Classical Legends — 20
The Renaissance — 22
Science and Alchemy — 24
Age of Enlightenment — 26
Masonic Ritual — 28
Past into Present — 30

Part Three

MASONIC ARCHITECTURE — 32

Architecture — 34
Solomon's Temple — 36
Egyptian Influences — 38
Classical Architecture — 40
Masonic Buildings — 42
The Lodge Interior — 44
Gardens — 46

Part Four

SIGNS AND SYMBOLS — 48

The Working Tools — 50
The Symbolic Temple — 52
The Great Pyramid — 54
Solomon's Columns — 56
The All-Seeing Eye — 58
Sun and Blazing Star — 60
The Moon — 62
The Globes — 64
The Mosaic Pavement — 66
Stairs and Ladders — 68
The Coffin and Skull — 70
Swords and Daggers — 72
Geometric Shapes — 74
Symbolic Cities — 76
Book, Bees and Beehive — 78
Life, Time and Justice — 80
Wheat and Plants — 82
The Jewels — 84
The Pentagram — 86
The Apron — 88
Tracing Boards — 90

Glossary — 92

Index — 94

Bibliography — 96

PART ONE

INTRODUCING FREEMASONRY

 Freemasonry is the oldest and largest fraternal organization in the world. Put at its simplest, it is a universal society of friends who seek to become better people through their association with one another. Its watchwords are fellowship, integrity and good citizenship. Its origins, however, are obscure. Some trace the beginning of Freemasonry to the master masons who created the great churches and cathedrals of medieval Europe; some argue that its birth was linked to the Knights Templar, a military and religious order of warrior-knights who rose to prominence at the time of the Crusades. Others say that Freemasonry's roots go further back than that – to the time of King Solomon and the building of his great temple in Jerusalem, if not before.

RIGHT A fifteenth-century woodcut depicting the Old Testament story of building the Tower of Babel. The enterprise was believed to have been planned by Masons.

IDEAS AND IDEALS

FREEMASONRY IS NOT A RELIGION, THOUGH MANY CHRISTIAN IDEAS AND IDEALS ARE IMPORTANT TO MASONS. IT IS WHAT MASONS TERM A FRATERNAL ORDER, WHOSE BASIC TENETS ARE BROTHERLY LOVE AND RELIEF. BROTHERLY LOVE REQUIRES THAT MASONS BE TOLERANT, RESPECTFUL, KIND AND UNDERSTANDING. RELIEF REFERS TO THE ACTIVE PRACTICE OF CHARITY AND COMMITMENT TO OTHER FORMS OF PHILANTHROPY, AND TRUTH. THE ESSENTIAL QUALIFICATION ALL MASONS MUST SHARE IS A BELIEF IN A SINGLE SUPREME BEING. MEMBERSHIP, THEREFORE, IS OPEN TO PEOPLE OF ANY RACE OR RELIGION WHO CAN FULFIL THIS QUALIFICATION AND ARE "OF GOOD CHARACTER AND REPUTE".

BELOW The values of Freemasonry personified in a French lithograph. It symbolizes the belief that self-improvement paves the way to enlightenment.

Being a Freemason means possessing a belief that there is a divine intelligence that governs the working of the universe. Freemasonry has no doctrines or dogmas as such, or any political or

religious affiliations. Rather, it is a system of morality, which is veiled heavily in allegory and illustrated by symbols, with implications for a way of living that leads to self-improvement through service to the world. The Masonic argument is that these are the surest ways by which moral and ethical truths may be taught. It is compatible with various world-views and religious and philosophical traditions without being limited to any one of them.

THE GROWTH OF MASONIC RITUAL

Much of the ritual that surrounds Freemasonry has grown up over the centuries. To the uninitiated many of the rituals appear to have come from obscure traditions. It is evident, for instance, that Freemasonry relies heavily on notions gleaned from the customs and practices of the stonemasons of medieval times. It is undoubtedly from stonemasonry that the Square and the Compasses — two of the best known of all Masonic symbols — derive. Together with the Bible, these make up the three Great Lights of Freemasonry in Christian countries. Elsewhere, the appropriate volume of Sacred Law replaces the Bible.

Arguably, the most important of the Square's many meanings — with its immovable legs set at 90° — is that it represents matter. The Compasses,

which have movable adjustable legs, represent consciousness or spirit. Both are regularly shown in combination, suggesting that matter and consciousness are interdependent realities.

FROM MYTHOLOGY TO PRACTICE

Freemasonry revolves around the creation of an all-embracing central mythology. This mythology features heavily the building of King Solomon's Temple in Jerusalem as its central theme. Some Masons go even further than this view, suggesting that Freemasonry has highly charged symbolic links with other similar initiatory orders throughout human history – and sees itself as the chief modern form of the Ancient Mysteries.

In practice, Freemasonry operates on a number of levels – a fact recognized in the various degrees that members of a lodge have to pass through as they progress in Masonic knowledge. The overriding truth is that when you become a Mason, you commit yourself to exploring a unique design for living. Under the guidance that Freemasonry can provide, eventually you will reach the gateway that marks the beginning of the great journey along the path of self-discovery. By following this path to its logical conclusion, you will end up with a revelatory knowledge of your inner nature and understand the way in which you link harmoniously with all other life on the planet.

ABOVE In this illustration, Truth uses her mirror to light up Freemason's Hall, London. Companion figures symbolize faith, hope and charity.

ABOVE LEFT God Almighty, as depicted in the Cathedral of the Assumption, Moscow. Belief in the existence of a Supreme Being of any faith lies at the heart of Freemasonry.

ORIGINS AND ALLEGORIES

SOME FREEMASONS CLAIMED THAT THE ROOTS OF THE SOCIETY, IN COMMON WITH OTHER MYSTIC TRADITIONS, LIE FAR BACK IN ANCIENT EGYPT AND BIBLICAL ISRAEL. BUT MOST MASONIC SCHOLARS TODAY ACCEPT THAT THERE IS NO FIRM EVIDENCE FOR SUCH LINKS. THEY BELIEVE THAT FREEMASONRY IN ITS ORIGINAL FORM EVOLVED FROM THE MEDIEVAL STONEMASONS' GUILDS, OR THAT IT CAME ABOUT AS A RESULT OF A DISPERSAL OF KNOWLEDGE FOLLOWING THE SUPPRESSION OF THE QUASI-RELIGIOUS MILITARY ORDER KNOWN AS THE KNIGHTS TEMPLAR. WHATEVER THE TRUTH, CLEARLY FREEMASONRY DERIVES ITS RITES AND RITUALS FROM VARIOUS SOURCES — SOME MORE ARCANE THAN OTHERS.

BELOW The sacrifice of the Israelites on the site that was to become Jerusalem, where King Solomon's Temple was built. The tabernacle, housing the Ark of the Covenant, is depicted in the background.

It seems highly unlikely that the true origins of Freemasonry will ever be uncovered. The majority of Masons believe that the modern story of the movement began with the stonemasons, builders of Europe's greatest cathedrals. Member masons were craftsmen, who banded together to practise

what Masons today call "the operative art" of masonry. They were an elite class that could travel freely between countries – unlike serfs, whose movements were carefully controlled and closely restricted. Hence, the term "free mason" came into being.

PASSING ON KNOWLEDGE

The masons' guilds had two other important functions. In common with similar organizations of the time, they had additional specific responsibilities – the induction of suitable trainees as apprentices and the preservation of the secrets of their trade. Because the medieval world was steeped in religion, spiritual and ethical instruction was part and parcel of the apprentices' training, giving rise to the lessons that are incorporated in the Masonic degrees.

The various passwords and secret handgrips that form an integral part of Masonic ritual probably originated from Freemasonry's insistence on secrecy. Originally, these passwords and secret means of recognition were probably intended to help genuine operative masons to get work or other forms of aid when they were on the move, passing from one lodge to another.

The tools of stonemasonry – plumb line, square, compasses, level, chisel, mallet, trowel and gauge – also had an important role to play. In Freemasonry, they came to hold important symbolic meanings, epitomizing various moral and ethical virtues.

THE IMPORTANCE OF ALLEGORY

Allegories drawn from building play an extremely important part in the rites and rituals of Freemasonry. As initiate Masons progress through the various ceremonies, for instance, they learn that, at the building of King Solomon's Temple in Jerusalem, the masons who worked on the great project were divided into two classes – Apprentices and Fellows – and that they were presided over by three Grand Masters, one of

whom was Solomon himself. The others were Hiram, King of Tyre, and Hiram Abif, the temple's architect. The Grand Masters were the guardians of the ultimate secrets of what Masons term the Great Craft. The implication is that Freemasonry was already established in King Solomon's time and has continued unchanged ever since. The reality is that the rites and rituals associated with Freemasonry are not based on historical fact at all. Rather it is a dramatic allegory, through which important principles and tenets of Freemasonry are passed on from one generation to the next.

ABOVE The Mason to the left of the column in this fourteenth-century French depiction is holding a square and compass. Both are important Working Tools in Freemasonry.

ABOVE LEFT Masons are seen moving stone blocks in this sixteenth-century illustration. The Ashlars, as such stones are named in Freemasonry, have a major symbolic part to play in Masonic ritual.

MASONIC OATHS

To an outsider, the seemingly gruesome oaths Freemasons have to swear to protect their secrets are off-putting at best and irreligious at worst. This is simply not the case. The obligations contained in such oaths – notably those dispensed during the admission ceremonies to the Three Degrees – have always been strictly allegorical in character. In reality, the only penalties that can be imposed on a Mason by his fellows are those of reprimand, suspension or expulsion.

PART TWO

LEGEND AND HISTORY

 The traditions of Freemasonry are an eclectic mixture of mystical legend and historical fact. This is partly the result of a profound change in the nature of Freemasonry that came about in the eighteenth century, during the period of history known as the Enlightenment, when lodges began to accept members who were not stonemasons. Among their number were men like Wolfgang Amadeus Mozart, Johann Wolfgang von Goethe, Frederick the Great and George Washington. As a consequence of this, many lodges now dubbed themselves "speculative" rather than "operative", dealing in ideas and the formulation of ideals rather than stone. It is these ideals which govern Freemasonry today.

RIGHT An eighteenth-century illustration depicting Freemasons. On the wall are signs for the lodges that had started up since the Grand Lodge opened in London in 1717, when four lodges were united. By 1750 there were several hundred lodges in England.

THE KNIGHTS TEMPLAR

SINCE THE CREATION OF THE FIRST GRAND LODGE OF MODERN FREEMASONRY IN 1717, THERE HAS BEEN SPECULATION ABOUT FREEMASONRY'S HISTORICAL ROOTS. THE THEORIES HAVE BEEN VARIED, BUT ONE OF THE MOST INTRIGUING IS THAT FREEMASONRY BEGAN IN SCOTLAND IN THE EARLY FOURTEENTH CENTURY AND THAT IT OWED ITS FOUNDATION TO SURVIVORS OF THE KNIGHTS TEMPLAR, WHO FLED THERE FROM FRANCE AFTER THE SUPPRESSION OF THEIR ORDER. THERE, TO PROTECT THEMSELVES FROM DISCOVERY AND PERSECUTION, THEY ASSUMED THE TITLE OF FREEMASONS AND SO ENSURED THEIR SURVIVAL, ALBEIT UNDER ANOTHER NAME.

BELOW A nineteenth-century impression of tombs of the Knights Templar. The Order was a significant force in medieval Europe. According to Masonic tradition, some knights may have fled to Scotland, where they helped to found Scottish Freemasonry.

The Knights Templar were a monastic military order formed at the end of the First Crusade (1095–9) with the mandate of protecting Christian pilgrims on their journey to the Holy Land. Their beginnings were humble enough; they relied on alms from travelling pilgrims for survival. Yet within two centuries they had become rich and powerful enough to defy all but the Pope in Rome – indeed, Pope Innocent II (reigned 1130–43) had specifically released them from any obligation to obey any secular power.

It was their power – and the massive wealth they had amassed, largely through money-lending to kings – that brought about the Knights Templar's downfall. In 1307, having secured the support of Pope Clement V, Philip IV of France ordered the arrest of all known Templars on charges of heresy (their secret meetings and rituals offered him the perfect excuse). Seven years later, by which time the order had been dissolved, Jacques de Molay, its last Grand Master, was burned at the stake. The survivors scattered, their power seemingly broken for ever.

FROM HISTORY TO SPECULATION

So much is history. What followed – notably the claim that Templar survivors were the power behind the foundation of Freemasonry – is unverifiable speculation. There are other factors, however, which seem to support the notion of some degree of Templar involvement.

Though it is widely accepted that Freemasonry did originate in medieval Scotland, the reason for this is unclear. Scotland possessed only a few stonemasons' lodges, whereas continental Europe had many. It would be reasonable to suggest that Freemasonry would have originated in Europe, but

LEFT Rosslyn Chapel, Scotland, is thought to be modelled on Herod's Temple, and Knights Templar are said to have had a hand in its building.

FAR LEFT The Apprentice's Pillar in Rosslyn Chapel was supposedly the work of the Master Mason's apprentice. He was killed by his master in a fit of jealous rage at the perfection of the construction.

it is known that this was not the case. There is further evidence to support the Scottish link – the connection between Templars and Masons in Rosslyn Chapel, a few miles south of Edinburgh. Sir William St Clair built the chapel in 1440 to house artefacts originally brought to Scotland by the Knights Templar in 1126.

It has been suggested that the chapel was built as a replica of Herod's Temple in Jerusalem, which the Templars had excavated during their time in the Holy Land. Even more importantly, the chapel contains a unique carving, which some scholars are certain depicts the initiation of a Mason by a figure wearing a Knight Templar's mantle.

Unfortunately, what is lacking is indisputable historical proof. Although the link is disputed by many scholars, it is entirely possible that fugitive Templars were admitted into the fraternities of Scottish stonemasons.

THE ROSSLYN CONNECTION

Rosslyn Chapel's unique stone carvings makes it important in the story of Scottish Freemasonry. One of the carvings depicts the chapel's Master Mason, who, in an act resembling the murder of Hiram Abif (the architect of King Solomon's Temple) is said to have killed his apprentice in a fit of jealous rage following the latter's creation of the so called Apprentice's Pillar. This pillar is a representation of the Norse Tree of Knowledge, the Christian equivalent of which is the Tree of Life.

LEFT A Masonic Scottish badge of uncertain date celebrates the supposed link between early Freemasonry and the Knights Templar. The belief is that refugee Templars joined Scottish Operative Lodges.

LEGEND AND RITUAL

FOR FREEMASONS, LEGEND IS EXTREMELY IMPORTANT, ESPECIALLY WHEN IT COMES TO THE PRACTICE OF THE RITES, RITUALS AND MYSTERIES OF THE CRAFT. KING SOLOMON'S TEMPLE IS IMPORTANT BECAUSE MASONS SEE IT AS THE PRIME EXAMPLE OF DIVINE ARCHITECTURE. LINKS WITH ANCIENT EGYPT ARE ALSO CLAIMED. THERE ARE CLEAR PARALLELS BETWEEN THE LEGEND OF HIRAM ABIF, WHICH IS ANOTHER CENTRAL FEATURE IN MASONIC RITUAL, AND THE MUCH OLDER ONE OF ISIS AND OSIRIS. GREEK LEGEND, TOO, PLAYS ITS PART, NOT SURPRISINGLY SINCE MATHEMATICS, AND MORE SPECIFICALLY GEOMETRY, IS ANOTHER KEY MASONIC THEME.

THE LEGEND OF THE PILLARS

BELOW An Apron worn by a French eighteenth-century Master Mason. Note in particular the two columns, symbolizing Boaz and Jachin (as seen from the perspective of the Temple), the Temple itself, and the group of Masonic emblems in the foreground.

Pillars play a conspicuous part in Masonic ceremonies, the most significant of them being the two named pillars – Boaz and Jachin. According to Masonic legend, the original pillars were erected at the entrance to King Solomon's Temple, Boaz on the left of the porchway and Jachin on the right. Their purpose, it has been claimed, was to give divine legitimacy to the ruling dynasty; in Hebrew, Jachin means "for God will establish", while Boaz is a composite of two words, "bo" meaning "in him" and "az" meaning strength. The pillars were thus a testament to the power and might of God.

The pillars were cast of bronze. It is likely that they stood at least 3m/10ft tall. They were hollow – though the theory that they were used to house secret archives has long been discounted – and adorned with capitals in the shape of huge bowls, each 2m/7ft deep.

The bowls were ornately rimmed with two rows of pomegranates, while lily work also featured. Both have their own meaning in Freemasonry – the pomegranate symbolizes plenty, while the lily stands for the need for modesty and rectitude. The significance of Boaz in Freemasonry is revealed during First Degree initiation rites; that of Jachin during the rituals that mark the passage from First to Second Degree.

THE OLD CHARGES

The manuscripts and other documents collectively known as the Old Charges are also an important feature of the legendary traditions of Freemasonry. Masons regard knowledge of their contents as essential for an understanding of Masonic constitutional law and practice.

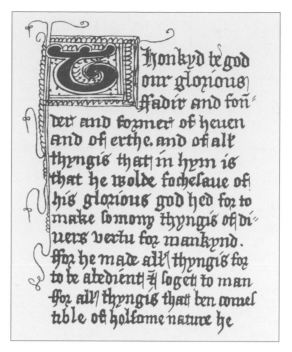

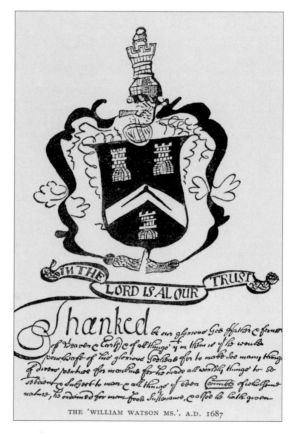

LEFT Pages from the Regius (far left) and Cook (left) manuscripts. They date from the end of the fourteenth and early fifteenth centuries and, together with other early documents, make up what Masons call the Old Charges.

The Old Charges all originated in England. The earliest – the Regius Manuscript and the Cook Manuscript – date from around 1390 and 1420 respectively. It is likely that the Cook Manuscript is the more authentic, since internal evidence suggests that a practising Mason wrote it. The bulk of the documents date from the late sixteenth to the early eighteenth centuries, starting with the Grand Lodge No. I Manuscript of December 1583. Historians have queried the authenticity of later documents, often regarded as antiquarian curiosities. The Regius Manuscript is in verse, the others in prose; apart from this difference, all have a more or less identical form. They start with an opening prayer, followed by a detailed history of Freemasonry, tracing its origins back to the days before the Flood and charting its growth and spread through the ages until its establishment in England in Saxon times. This is followed by a code of regulations for Master Masons, Fellow Masons and Apprentices, covering craft practices and morals, arrangements for large-scale assemblies, procedures for the trial and punishment of offenders and admissions procedures for "new men that were never charged before", including an oath of loyalty.

LEFT An extract from the "William Watson manuscript". This may be another important Masonic document, but historians query the authencity of some of the later records of Freemasonry. This manuscript is believed to be dated around 1687.

THE LEGEND OF ENOCH

How, when, why and where Freemasonry originated is a legend in its own right. It can be traced back to the time of Enoch, the seventh of the Hebrew patriarchs of the Old Testament and the great-grandfather of Noah. He is said to have initiated and promoted a Craft in which the eternal truths of Freemasonry were revealed through emblems, symbols, mystics and mysteries.

THE HIRAMIC LEGEND

THE LEGEND OF HIRAM ABIF, THE MASTER ARCHITECT OF KING SOLOMON'S TEMPLE, IS ONE OF THE CENTRAL ALLEGORIES IN FREEMASONRY. HIS MURDER AT THE HANDS OF THREE OF HIS SUBORDINATE CRAFTSMEN FOR REFUSING TO REVEAL THE SECRETS OF MASTER MASONRY, AND HIS SUBSEQUENT REBIRTH, DESCRIBED AS HIS RISE FROM "A DEAD LEVEL" TO "A LIVING PERPENDICULAR", IS A KEY PART OF THE RITUAL THAT MARKS THE PROGRESS OF A MASON FROM THE SECOND TO THE THIRD DEGREE.

BELOW A depiction of the death of Hiram Abif, King Solomon's master architect, murdered by his underlings for refusing to divulge the most hidden of Masonic secrets.

The story is as follows. Each day at noon – High Twelve, in Masonic parlance – Hiram Abif went into the temple to pray. Three of his subordinate craftsmen, who aspired to become Master Masons, lay in wait for him one day as he came out, their

plan being to force him to reveal the secret words of recognition. Upon his refusal, each of them attacked Abif in turn. Finally, he fell to the ground, dead. The murderers buried their victim, but a search party led by Solomon himself found the grave. Then, after Entered Apprentices and Fellow Craftsmen had failed to resurrect their master, Solomon, a fellow Master Mason, raised him with the "strong grip of a lion's paw".

The legend became part of Freemasonry between 1723 and 1738. It is clearly not history – it is a ritualistic drama, actually acted out in the lodge during the process of Third Degree initiation, in which the candidate plays the part of Hiram Abif. Through their participation in the ritual, candidates learn how the soul can rise above its internal enemies – ignorance, lust, passion and sin – so that they can become masters of themselves and their destinies.

THE MYSTERIES

According to the great Masonic scholar Albert Mackey, the legend of Hiram Abif was borrowed from what scholars term the Ancient Mysteries of early Egypt, Mesopotamia and Rome. This is described in Dr Albert G. Mackey's *Manual of the Lodge*, in which he argues that there is no biblical evidence that such a character ever existed and met his death in such a way. Rather than being part of any biblical tradition, Abif is the representative of the gods Osiris, Baal and Bacchus.

RIGHT A ceremonial sword of a type used in the initiation of a Master Mason. It is ornately detailed with symbolic emblems along much of the length of the blade.

BELOW Acting out the murder of Hiram Abif is central to the rituals governing admission to the Third Degree.

BOTTOM The candidate is raised after a symbolic death, where his face is covered and swords are pointed at his body.

This is by no means the only supposed link with the Ancient Mysteries. It is argued that the Compasses and Square, for instance, represent ancient pagan sun deities, while, like the sun temples of the ancient Middle East, Masonic temples are usually built on an east–west axis. Venturing slightly further ahead in time, Masonic writers have often claimed to see many resemblances between Freemasonry and Mithraism, the cult of the Persian god Mithras that eventually spread from its homeland to the Roman Empire itself.

The existence of direct and arcane links between Freemasonry and the Ancient Mysteries is disputed by many present-day Masons. While they admit there are similarities between their fraternity and the old mystery cults – just like Freemasonry, Mithraism featured elaborate initiation rites for its various successive degrees – Masons point out that most of the similarities are superficial in character. In the main, Masons are concerned with the externals of rite or organization rather than deeper content.

MITHRAISM AND MASONRY

Nineteenth-century Masonic writer Albert Pike declared that Freemasonry was "the modern heir" of the Ancient Mysteries, and Sir Samuel Dill described Mithraism as "a sacred Freemasonry". There are certainly similarities. Like Freemasonry, Mithraism was divided into grades, each of which had its own symbolic ceremonies to mark initiation. As in Masonry, the practice of charity was important, while, like Masons, Mithraists greeted one another with the word "brother".

CLASSICAL LEGENDS

EGYPT HAS ALWAYS BEEN CONSIDERED TO BE THE BIRTHPLACE OF THE MYSTERIES. IT WAS IN EGYPT THAT CEREMONIES OF INITIATION WERE FIRST ESTABLISHED, TRUTH WAS FIRST VERSED IN ALLEGORY, AND THE DOGMAS OF RELIGION WERE FIRST IMPARTED IN SYMBOLIC FORMS. SOME BELIEVE THAT THE LEGEND OF HIRAM ABIF IS BASED ON THE SUPPOSED FATE OF THE EGYPTIAN GOD OSIRIS. THOTH, THE ANCIENT EGYPTIAN GOD OF WISDOM, PLAYED A MAJOR PART IN PRESERVING THE KNOWLEDGE OF THE MASONS' CRAFT AND TRANSMITTING IT TO FUTURE GENERATIONS. GREECE HAS ALSO BEEN ASSOCIATED WITH SYMBOLISM – THROUGH THE ANCIENT ELEUSINIAN MYSTERIES AND GREEK FIGURES SUCH AS PYTHAGORAS.

BELOW The tombs of the kings outside Thebes demonstrate how important hieroglyphs were in ancient Egypt. Freemasonry borrowed from such traditions.

BELOW RIGHT According to some Masonic scholars, Isis, the Egyptian goddess of fertility, and her husband Osiris are linked to the origins of Freemasonry.

LEARNING FROM THE EGYPTIANS

Much of Masonic architecture and formal dress – notably the Masonic Apron – is indebted to ancient Egyptian precedents. Unfortunately, no amount of research has yet been able to establish any causal link between the two. We do know, however, that in ancient Egypt the architects and craftsmen who worked on that civilization's monumental building projects, such as the pyramids, were accorded a special status in contemporary society. Additionally, they were organized into guilds. Evidence for this comes from papyrus records, one of which describes a guild that held secret meetings in around 2000BC. Its members met to discuss working conditions, wages and rules for daily labour. They also provided charitable relief to workers' widows and orphans, and to workers in distress. The parallel between

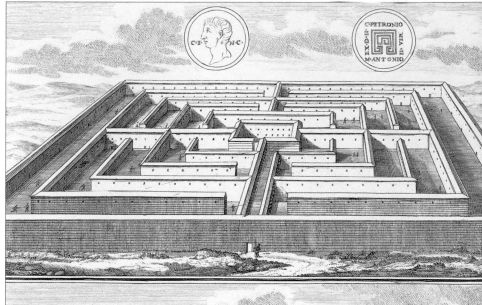

the kind of organizational duties described in the papyrus and those of a Warden or Master in a Freemasons' lodge is strong. However, this may be nothing more than coincidence, and it is unlikely that anyone will ever be able to establish the truth.

LEARNING FROM THE GREEKS

Just as they looked towards ancient Egypt, some Freemasons historically thought that the culture and civilization of ancient Greece contributed to the development of Masonic rites and ritual. The ancient Eleusinian Mysteries – so called because they were celebrated at Eleusis, near Athens – have parallels with the Masonic commemoration of Hiram Abif's martyrdom, but, again, this is probably no more than coincidental.

One major Greek figure traditionally associated with Freemasonry is undoubtedly Pythagoras, an Ionian Greek who was probably born in around 570BC on the island of Samos and rose to become one of the most celebrated mathematicians of all time. He founded his own secret society, the Pythagoreans, among whom the pentagram, or five-pointed star, was a symbol of health and knowledge. The sign also became associated with rites of initiation, just as it is in Masonic iconography – often appearing on Masonic

regalia, such as the jewels of office worn by the Masters of Lodges and Grand Masters of Grand Lodges, and in decorative illustration. One reason for its appearance may be that it can be interpreted as a representation of the Golden Ratio, knowledge of which is vital for all architects and builders.

Some Masons believe another Greek figure is linked to Freemasonry's origins: the inventor-craftsman Daedalus, who designed the Cretan labyrinth for King Minos to house the legendary Minotaur. Daedalus is said to be the inventor of a number of the tools used in the various degrees of Freemasonry – notably the plumb line – while Perdix, his nephew, is the reputed inventor of the compasses, Freemasonry's third Great Light.

THE ELEUSINIAN MYSTERIES

Of all the mysteries celebrated in ancient times, the Eleusinian ones were considered to be the greatest in importance. They were basically initiation ceremonies for the cult of Demeter, the Greek goddess of life, agriculture and fertility, and Persephone, her daughter. The mysteries celebrated Persephone's reunion with her mother after Hades, the god of the underworld, had kidnapped her.

ABOVE The labyrinth built by Daedalus for King Minos of Crete. Some Masons think that Daedalus was an early proponent of the Craft.

ABOVE LEFT The Sphinx and the Great Pyramid were built by skilled craftsmen who may have been proto-Masons.

ABOVE In Greek legend Daedalus and his son, Icarus, flee Minoan Crete. Icarus paid with his life when he ignored his father's advice and flew too close to the sun. The wax that held his wings together melted and he fell from the skies.

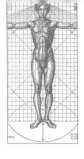

THE RENAISSANCE

WITH THE COMING OF THE RENAISSANCE, WESTERN EUROPEAN SOCIETY WENT THROUGH A SERIES OF RADICAL CHANGES. IN AROUND 1450, A PLATONIC ACADEMY WAS FOUNDED IN FLORENCE — AND IN 1471 A LATIN TRANSLATION OF THE RECENTLY REDISCOVERED GREEK *CORPUS HERMETICUM* APPEARED. IT WAS TO PROVE IMMENSELY INFLUENTIAL. FREEMASONRY HAD ALREADY RECOGNIZED THE IMPORTANCE OF ANCIENT KNOWLEDGE. IT NOW SHARED IN THE HERMETIC QUEST FOR LOST WISDOMS.

Like many other thinkers, the Masons dreamed of greater freedom of thought, and political and religious reform. Given the climate of the times, when many governments and the Catholic Church fiercely opposed such radical thinking, it was hardly surprising that its activities now came to be conducted in secrecy.

The nature of Freemasonry itself went through a transformation during this turbulent period. The impetus for this came from Scotland, where in 1583 King James VI and I appointed Sir William Schaw, a Scottish nobleman with a passionate interest in architecture, as Master of the Work and Warden General. In 1598 Schaw issued the first of the celebrated statutes which set out the duties that Masons owed to their lodges. The second statute, issued in 1599, is the first Masonic document that had survived to make veiled reference to the existence of esoteric knowledge within the Craft. The new spirit of the Renaissance was obviously having its impact, enabling Schaw to revive and develop medieval Masonic mythology and rituals. In Scotland, Freemasonry appeared to have royal backing. According to William Preston in his *Illustrations of Masonry* (1772), James became "the patron of the learned and zealous encourager of Masonry".

LEFT James VI and I depicted with his wife Anne of Denmark. James was a staunch supporter of Freemasonry.

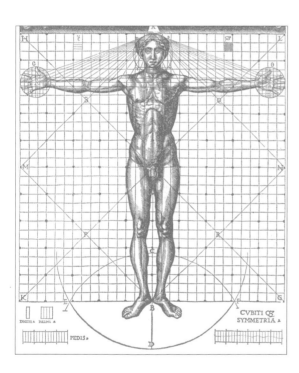

Scottish records relate that "he honoured the lodges with his royal presence" and that "he settled a yearly revenue of four pounds Scots to be paid by every Master Mason to a Grand Master chosen by the Grand Lodge and approved by the Crown". James was also the first king known to be a Freemason and was initiated into the Lodge of Scots and Perth in 1601 at the age of 35.

The earliest known record of a Masonic initiation anywhere is that of John Boswell, the Laird of Auchenleck, who was initiated into the Lodge of Edinburgh in June the preceding year.

Thus the scene was set for the further transformation of Freemasonry that was to gather momentum during the seventeenth century, though just how or when the transition from Operative Masonry to Intellectual Masonry took place is not clear. We do know, however, that as the guild system began to break down, what is known as Operative Masonry started to evolve into what is termed Speculative Masonry. Eventually the operative side was to be lost altogether with Masons being drawn chiefly from the nobility and the rising bourgeoisie.

ABOVE A seventeenth-century notion of an astrologer's costume. The beginnings of modern science were closely linked with those of Speculative Freemasonry.

ABOVE LEFT A letter from Sir William Schaw, Master of Work to James VI and I. A Mason himself, Schaw played a leading part in organizing and expanding Scottish Freemasonry.

LEFT The notion of ideal proportions became an important Masonic principle.

SCIENCE AND ALCHEMY

THE SEVENTEENTH CENTURY WAS A TIME OF GREAT POLITICAL UPHEAVAL AND SOCIAL CHANGE. IN BRITAIN CHARLES I WAS BEHEADED; ON THE EUROPEAN CONTINENT, BITTER RELIGIOUS WAR WAGED FOR 30 YEARS. FREEMASONRY GREW APACE, CLOSELY LINKED TO THE EMERGENCE OF A NEW GENERATION OF SCIENTISTS AND SAVANTS, WHO BECAME ASSOCIATED WITH THE MOVEMENT AS IT EXPANDED. MASONRY BECAME SO FASHIONABLE THAT, AS THE CENTURY PROGRESSED, ACCEPTANCE MEMBERS (THE COLLECTIVE TERM FOR NON-OPERATIVE MASONS) BECAME THE MAJORITY IN MANY MASONIC LODGES.

BELOW Astronomers search the heavens for stars and planets. Many of the emerging generation of new scientists were Freemasons.

Scientists such as Robert Boyle, Christopher Wren and Isaac Newton were all early members of the Royal Society, which had begun life as a quasi-Masonic institution called the Invisible College. In its early years, the Royal Society often held meetings in the Compton Room at Canonbury

Tower in north London. The room is decorated with carvings of Masonic significance. They were commissioned by Francis Bacon, a Mason and one of the Invisible College's founder leaders. A champion of inductive reasoning, Bacon has often been described as "the father of modern science".

In its early days, the proceedings of the Invisible College were cloaked in secrecy, as these were times of fear, state control and relative intolerance. Galileo, one of its founders, was condemned by the Catholic Church for daring to suggest that the earth revolved around the sun. Personal safety probably demanded that discussion of anything of an esoteric, moral or scientific nature took place underground. It seems more than probable that those seeking a vehicle in which they could discuss what the outside world might regard as dangerous ideas and beliefs freely would turn to Freemasonry. What emerged as a result was a new Speculative form of the Craft, which merely bore an allegorical likeness to the earlier Operative traditions.

OLD BELIEFS, NEW SCIENCE

Past beliefs intermingled with the new as much in science as in Freemasonry. Elias Ashmole, who was one of the first recorded inductees into English Freemasonry, was initiated as a Mason in Warrington, Lancashire, in 1646. He was a founder member of the Royal Society and stands as a good example of how old arcane beliefs and the new science could coexist. In 1652 Ashmole published his *Theatrum Chemicum Britannicum*, a compilation of all the writings on alchemy that had been produced by English authors, including those of Dr John Dee, the great Elizabethan savant and reputed magician. It should not be forgotten that, at this time, men of science still believed in the possibility of the transmutation of base metals into gold, the notion of a possible Elixir of Life, and other arcane beliefs. Newton himself spent a great deal of time trying to calculate the date of the end of the world.

For Freemasonry, the branch of science of greatest interest was undoubtedly geometry. Knowledge of geometry was an essential part of the Masonic tradition. Masons now came to believe that such knowledge would make it possible to recognize the principles upon which nature and society were built.

LEFT An alchemist's laboratory. The search for the Philosopher's Stone and the Elixir of Life were part of a quest for knowledge that fitted in well with the most important of Masonic principles.

ABOVE Lawyer and philosopher Sir Francis Bacon was James VI and I's Lord Chancellor and a leading light of the Invisible College. This was the precursor of the Royal Society.

LEFT Alchemy, with its arcane beliefs, slowly transmuted into modern chemistry. Freemasons were interested in all the new sciences, most notably that of geometry.

WAS SIR FRANCIS BACON A FREEMASON?

Though many have claimed that Sir Francis Bacon was a Freemason, there is no hard historical evidence to show that he was ever formally initiated into the Brotherhood. What is known is that he actively encouraged the setting up of the Mason's Hall in London as the model for an allegorical "Solomon's House", the inspiration for which came from Bacon's celebrated tract *The New Atlantis*.

AGE OF ENLIGHTENMENT

THE EIGHTEENTH CENTURY MARKED MAJOR NEW BEGINNINGS FOR FREEMASONRY. FOUR LODGES
BANDED TOGETHER IN 1721 TO FORM THE PREMIER GRAND LODGE IN LONDON. IN 1731 THE
GRAND LODGE OF PENNSYLVANIA, THE FIRST GRAND LODGE TO BE FOUNDED IN WHAT WOULD LATER
BECOME THE USA, OBTAINED ITS CONSTITUTION; BY THE END OF THAT DECADE, THERE WERE LODGES IN
BELGIUM, RUSSIA, ITALY, GERMANY AND SWITZERLAND. FIVE LODGES WERE FOUNDED IN PARIS BY 1742.

BELOW A seventeenth-
century illustration
records humanity's
progress in the
sciences, including
those of geometry
and architecture.
Both are central to
Masonic thinking.

Freemasonry stood for rationalism, deism and
benevolence – three of the most important
characteristics of the Enlightenment ideas and
ideals that were swiftly coming to prominence.
What differed was the way in which these ideals
were interpreted and applied. According to
Michael Baigant and Richard Leigh's *The Temple
and the Lodge*, as early as the 1730s, Freemasonry in
England was fast becoming a pillar of the social

and cultural establishment. It fostered a spirit of
moderation, tolerance and flexibility, and often
worked hand in hand with the established church.
Many clergymen became Freemasons themselves.
There was a major rift within Freemasonry in
1751, however, when the so called Ancients broke
away from the Moderns of the existing Grand
Lodge. The former were so called because they
believed that they adhered more faithfully to

L'ACADEMIE DES SCIENCES ET DES BEAUX ARTS
DEDIEE
AU ROY.
Par son tres humble tres obeissant et tres fidele Serviteur et sujet Seb. le Clerc.

traditional Masonic ritual, passwords and customs. The breach between the Ancients and Moderns was not healed until 1813, when the United Grand Lodge of England was formed.

In Catholic Europe, on the other hand, Freemasonry just as quickly became identified with militant anticlerical, anti-establishment and eventually revolutionary ideas. In France, for instance, prominent Freemasons, such as the Marquis de Lafayette, Georges Danton and Emmanuel-Joseph Sieyès, were prime movers in the overthrow of the Bourbon monarchy in the Revolution of 1789. These leaders believed they were acting in full accordance with Masonic ideals.

THE AMERICAN REVOLUTION

It is likely that the first native-born American to be made a Mason was Jonathan Belcher, the governor of Massachusetts, in 1703, and the Order soon grew in power and influence. Freemasons played a significant part in the events leading up to the Declaration of Independence

and the subsequent struggle to free the American colonies from British rule. William Bramley in *The Gods of Eden* claims that a Masonic lodge – St Andrew's Lodge in Boston – was the prime mover in the Boston Tea Party of 1773, for instance, while Michael Baigent et al. in *The Messianic Legacy* argues that most of the men responsible for creating the USA "were staunch Freemasons" and that "the new nation was originally conceived as the ideal hierarchic political structure postulated by certain Masonic rites".

What is known for a fact is that of the five men appointed by the Continental Congress to draft the Declaration of Independence, two were Masons, as were 19 signatories of the Declaration itself. They included George Washington, Benjamin Franklin and John Hancock, the president of the Congress. Franklin was Provincial Grand Master of Philadelphia and visited lodges in England, Scotland and France. He was the American publisher of the *Constitutions of the Freemasons*, which had been drawn up in the 1720s.

ABOVE The composer Mozart (seated extreme left) at a Viennese initiation ceremony.

BELOW George Washington, founding father of the United States, was an active Mason for most of his life.

MASONIC RITUAL

IT WAS IN THE 1720S, SHORTLY AFTER THE FOUNDING OF THE FIRST GRAND LODGE IN ENGLAND, THAT THE MASONIC RITUAL OF INITIATION WAS CLARIFIED INTO A SYSTEM BASED ON THREE DEGREES, OR LEVELS. IN THE EARLY DAYS OF FREEMASONRY, THERE HAD BEEN ONLY TWO DEGREES. NOW A THIRD ONE WAS ADDED, FOLLOWED LATER BY THE ROYAL ARCH DEGREE. IN BLUE LODGE MASONRY, THE PROCESS ENDS THERE. HOWEVER, ANY MASTER MASON (SOMEONE WHO HAS BEEN INITIATED INTO THE THIRD DEGREE) IS ELIGIBLE TO JOIN THE YORK RITE, WHICH HAS NINE FURTHER DEGREES, OR SCOTTISH RITE (UP TO 32 DEGREES). A 33RD DEGREE MASON OF THE SCOTTISH RITE IS AN HONORARY POSITION.

THE FIRST DEGREE

Of the Three Degrees, the first is that of an Entered Apprentice. The initiation begins when the "hoodwinked" (blindfolded) and specially dressed candidate is brought before the entrance to the inner part of the temple and a guard hits the door with his sword hilt. After questions as to his eligibility and whether his motives are "worthy", and a short prayer, he is led three times around the meeting room, pausing on each lap to be introduced as "a poor candidate in a state of darkness". He is then brought before the Worshipful Master's pedestal (the Worshipful Master is the leader of the lodge) where he is asked: "What is the predominant wish of your heart?" The answer —"Light"— is whispered to

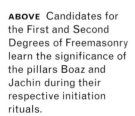

ABOVE Candidates for the First and Second Degrees of Freemasonry learn the significance of the pillars Boaz and Jachin during their respective initiation rituals.

RIGHT Masons assemble to initiate an Entered Apprentice. In this eighteenth-century depiction the Master of the Lodge is questioning the candidate before he reveals the secrets of the First Degree to him.

him and the blindfold removed. The Three Lights – the volume of Sacred Law (such as the Bible), the Square and the Compasses – are then revealed, followed by an explanation of the secret signs, grips and passwords of the First Degree and the meaning of Boaz, the left-hand pillar in King Solomon's Temple. It ends with the presentation of a Masonic Apron to the initiated candidate.

THE SECOND AND THIRD DEGREES

The Second Degree is that of Fellow Craft Mason. The candidate is admitted to the temple just as he was during his First Degree initiation, following which he has to recite answers to a number of questions that he has memorized. Among other things, these introduce him to "the hidden mysteries of science and nature", which he is now expected to study. He is again led around the temple, new signs and passwords are explained, and he learns the meaning of Jachin, the right-hand pillar of King Solomon's Temple.

The Third Degree – "the cement of the whole" according to the ritual – is that of Master Mason. Having answered more test questions successfully, the candidate enters the temple, which is in pitch darkness. After a prayer and a ceremony that resembles those of the first two degrees, the Worshipful Master and his fellow Masons act out the story of Hiram Abif, with the initiate playing the part of Hiram and his fellow Masons his murderers. It is the Worshipful Master who eventually raises the candidate to his feet, after which the initiate kneels before the altar and, resting his hands on the Three Lights, takes the Master Mason's oath.

ABOVE Little is known about the life of Anthony Sayer, who was elected the first Grand Master of the Grand Lodge of England in 1717.

BELOW Eighteenth-century Masons initiating a Master Mason, the third and highest of the Three Degrees of Freemasonry. The lit candles signify the approaching end of the ritual as the initiate passes from darkness to light.

MASONIC MONITORS

To help to understand rituals, many Masons rely on small books called Monitors, which explain the meanings of the major Masonic symbols and the important parts of the ritual itself.

PAST INTO PRESENT

IN SOME WAYS, THE NINETEENTH CENTURY WAS A HIGH WATERMARK FOR FREEMASONRY, YET IT ALSO CONTAINED THE SEEDS OF A PARTIAL DECLINE. IN EUROPE THERE WERE FURTHER SPLITS IN THE MOVEMENT, NOTABLY BETWEEN THE FRENCH FREEMASONS AND THEIR ENGLISH AND AMERICAN CONTEMPORARIES FROM 1877 ONWARDS. THE CHIEF REASON FOR THE RIFT WAS THE DECISION OF THE FRENCH GRAND LODGE OF THE ORIENT TO START ACCEPTING ATHEISTS AS INITIATES. THE FRENCH RECOGNITION OF WOMEN'S MASONRY ADDED FUEL TO THE FLAMES, AS DID THE WILLINGNESS OF FRENCH FREEMASONRY TO BECOME ACTIVELY INVOLVED IN MAJOR POLITICAL AND RELIGIOUS ISSUES.

BELOW Initiating a woman into Freemasonry in France in the mid-nineteenth century. The introduction of this practice led to a split between French Freemasonry and Masonry as practised in England and Scotland which has never been healed.

There was also the growth of anti-Masonic feeling to consider. In the USA, this began during the 1820s and led to the foundation of the Anti-Masonic Party in 1827. The party even fielded its own candidate for president against Andrew Jackson, who himself was a Mason. The growth of such feelings led to a change in Masonic thinking and direction. In response to

political and religious criticism, American Masonry turned inward, emphasizing spiritual values as opposed to its earlier, more public espousal of Enlightenment ideas. The lodge became a sanctuary that men could repair to for solace and inspiration.

Anti-Masonic feelings were not confined to the USA – in Catholic Europe they were just

as strong, if not stronger. The Catholic Church had been opposed to Freemasonry ever since 1738, when Pope Clement XII officially condemned it. In 1825 Pope Leo XII reiterated the condemnation, while in 1884 Pope Leo XIII called on Catholics everywhere "to strive for the extermination of this foul plague".

The papacy might have had practical as well as spiritual reasons for this blanket condemnation. The whole of the campaign leading to the political unification of Italy – to which the popes were vehemently opposed – could be described as essentially Masonic in inspiration. Indeed, two of the leading members of the Risorgimento – Giuseppe Mazzini and Giuseppe Garibaldi – were Freemasons. Mazzini was Past Grand Master of the Orient of Italy.

In France in the late nineteenth century, Freemasonry was violently attacked by the religious right, at the height of the Dreyfus Affair of the 1890s in which Alfred Dreyfus, a Jewish General Staff Officer, was falsely accused of selling secrets to the Germans. The Dreyfus Affair was seen by Catholic pro-military right-wingers as a conspiracy by Jews and Freemasons to damage the prestige of the army and of France.

FREEMASONRY AND TOTALITARIANISM

With the rise of totalitarian dictatorships in the twentieth century Freemasonry met its greatest challenge. In 1925 it was outlawed in Fascist Italy – the Masons were accused of involvement in a conspiracy to murder Benito Mussolini. After Adolf Hitler came to power in Germany in 1933, all Masonic lodges were suppressed, and many Masons were sent to concentration camps. It is estimated that some 200,000 Masons perished in the Holocaust.

FREEMASONRY TODAY

Today, there are around six million active Masons around the world, about half of them in the USA, which is the real powerhouse of modern Freemasonry. The Craft survives and continues to flourish. For more than three centuries, it has inspired millions of people across many countries. It has attracted many famous initiates – from Winston Churchill and Franklin Delano Roosevelt to Edward VIII and Ronald Reagan. Provided that Freemasonry moves with the times and explains its positive purpose effectively, there seems little reason to doubt that it will continue to prosper.

LEFT The King of Sweden initiated Edward VII of England as a Mason in 1868 during the latter's visit to Stockholm. According to a contemporary, Edward never lost "an opportunity to publicly show his attachment to the Masonic Fraternity".

ABOVE A Masonic emblem commemorating the death of a prominent Freemason, who was "near to the throne, but nearer to his fellow man".

BELOW Though attendance at lodge meetings is not compulsory, it is considered important – hence the admonitory "Fail not" at the foot of this eighteenth-century invitation.

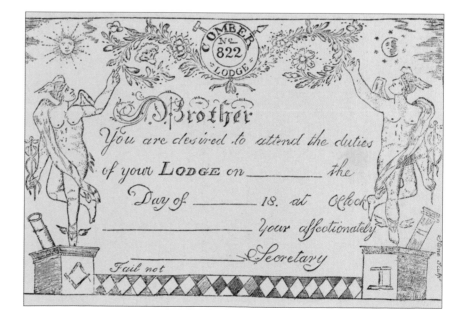

PART THREE

MASONIC ARCHITECTURE

 All Masons believe in a Supreme Being, typically referred to as "the Great Architect of the Universe". So it is not surprising that metaphor drawn from architecture features prominently in Masonic symbolism. Such metaphors serve to teach basic moral rules. A Perfect Ashlar, for instance, is a stone that has been hewn, smoothed and polished so as to be fit for use in building. In Masonic ritual, it is a symbol of the state of perfection that can be attained by means of education. In contrast, a Rough Ashlar, an unworked stone, is a symbol of man's natural state of ignorance. In some lodges, a newly initiated apprentice is asked to symbolically chip away a piece of the Rough Ashlar, to signify that his learning has begun.

RIGHT The Cathedral of Bourges is the largest of the three great French Gothic cathedrals, built between the late twelfth and early thirteenth centuries. Operative Masons would have been involved in the construction of this and other large cathedrals such as Chartres and Amiens.

ARCHITECTURE

ACCORDING TO ALBERT MACKEY IN *THE SYMBOLISM OF FREEMASONRY*, "ARCHITECTURE IS TO FREEMASONRY THE *ARS ATRIUM*, THE ART OF ARTS", SINCE MUCH OF THE SYMBOLISM THAT IS SUCH AN IMPORTANT PART OF MASONIC RITE AND RITUAL IS DRAWN FROM IT. IN SPECULATIVE FREEMASONRY, FOR INSTANCE, THE SPIRITUAL RELATIONSHIP BETWEEN THE CRAFT AND ARCHITECTURE FAR EXCEEDS THAT OF THE WORKING TOOLS AS SYMBOLS OR EVEN THAT OF GEOMETRY, IMPORTANT THOUGH BOTH OF THESE ARE IN MASONIC TRADITION. ITS STUDY IS THEREFORE AN INTEGRAL PART OF FREEMASONRY; ARCHITECTURE IS PART OF THE SEVEN "LIBERAL ARTS AND SCIENCES" TAUGHT IN THE FELLOW CRAFT DEGREE.

RIGHT Stained glass in Westminster Abbey, London, enclosed in a pointed arch. This is a classic example of Gothic architecture in which the Operative Masons of medieval times excelled.

BELOW Pillars in Westminster Abbey. Dr Albert G. Mackey claimed, "Gothic architecture has justly been called 'the architecture of Freemasonry'."

There is symbolism in Masonic architecture and also, more generally, in architecture with which Masons have been involved. In the Middle Ages, when the first Operative Lodges of stonemasons began to emerge, for instance, such symbolism demonstrated itself in the planning and building of the great churches and cathedrals, of which Chartres Cathedral in France probably stands as the foremost example.

In common with the majority of European cathedrals of the medieval period, Chartres is chiefly composed of simple geometric patterns that are repeated and elaborated to form the complex structure of the whole. At the same time, they give the impression of simplicity, balance and harmony. It seems more than likely that early Operative Masons were employed on the site.

The design employs various Masonic elements – these include the proportions of three, four and five (those of the perfect Pythagorean right angle) and the square, the circle and the rectangle squared at one end with a semicircle at the other. Of the three "tables" carved in the floor, the rectangular one has the same proportions as those of King Solomon's Temple, the length being twice the breadth.

Five- and seven-pointed stars also feature. In Freemasonry, the seven points of the latter represent the seven "liberal arts and sciences"

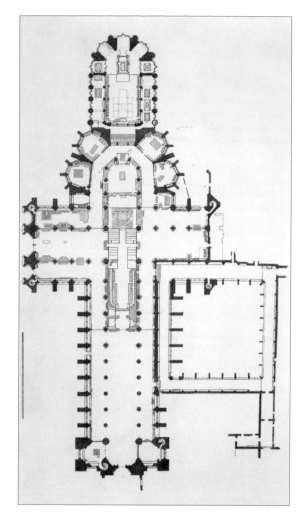

(grammar, rhetoric, dialectic, arithmetic, geometry, astronomy and music) that form the basis of Masonic education in the quest for knowledge and enlightenment. There is also a labyrinth, through which the devout could make a symbolic pilgrimage by following the convoluted path on their knees. Subsequently, the labyrinth has featured in purely Masonic outdoor architecture since the eighteenth century.

PLANNING AND ORDER

For Masons, architecture means to construct according to design and purpose and to organize in proportion and symmetry. It continues to be architecture, regardless of whether it is a building that is being constructed, as in Operative Masonry, or a human life that is being planned, as in Speculative Masonry. According to Masonic belief, the science of how an actual building was

constructed provides wisdom as to how to build a spiritual temple within one's own soul and collectively for the whole of mankind. This is why Masons have always revered the notion of order in architecture. Everything fits into a plan. It also partly explains the Masonic fascination with King Solomon's Temple, whose architecture and geometry were seen as perfect, and the ongoing importance of the temple in Masonic ritual.

ABOVE Chartres Cathedral is a masterpiece of medieval Gothic architecture. Operative Masons played a major role in its planning and construction.

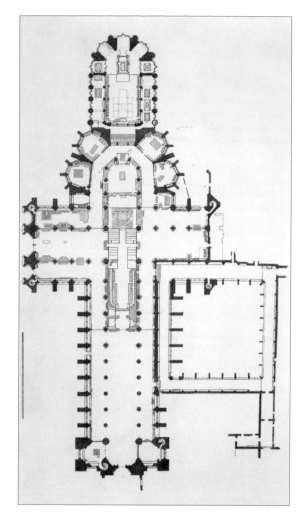

ABOVE LEFT The plan of a large church is conceived as the result of generations of practical and evolving building experience.

OPERATIVE AND SPECULATIVE

In the rituals governing admission to the Fellow Craft or Second Degree of Freemasonry, both Operative and Speculative Masonry are clearly defined. Put at its simplest, Operative Masonry involves the creation of physical architecture, while Speculative Masonry is the practice of human architecture. The links between the two date back to the earliest days of Freemasonry, when every member was an Operative Mason first and a Speculative one second. Over the years the emphasis changed, and today it has been completely reversed.

SOLOMON'S TEMPLE

ONE BELIEF ONCE SHARED BY ALL MASONS WAS THAT THE ROOTS OF THE CRAFT DATED BACK TO THE BUILDING OF KING SOLOMON'S TEMPLE IN JERUSALEM. IT WAS THE TASK OF THE CRAFT, THEY THOUGHT, TO RECONSTRUCT THE ORIGINAL PROPORTIONS OF THIS "MORAL EDIFICE". ALL LODGES ARE, OR OUGHT TO BE, SITUATED DUE EAST AND WEST, BECAUSE KING SOLOMON'S TEMPLE WAS SO SITUATED. EVEN THOUGH THE LINKS BETWEEN FREEMASONRY AND THE TEMPLE CANNOT BE SUBSTANTIATED, ITS PLACE IN CRAFT MYTHOLOGY REMAINS SECURE, AND MUCH MASONIC RITUAL STILL REVOLVES AROUND IT.

BELOW An eighteenth-century illustration shows what people thought King Solomon's Temple looked like, until destroyed by the Babylonians 400 years after it was built.

There is no doubt that the temple was an imposing building. According to Biblical scholars, King Solomon began its construction in 957BC, during the fourth year of his long reign, and it took seven years to build. It was surrounded by

high walls built of stone and timber, with an inner court inside extending from the temple proper. All around the temple were side chambers, arranged in three storeys. The entrance to the lowest was on the south side of the temple with stairs leading up

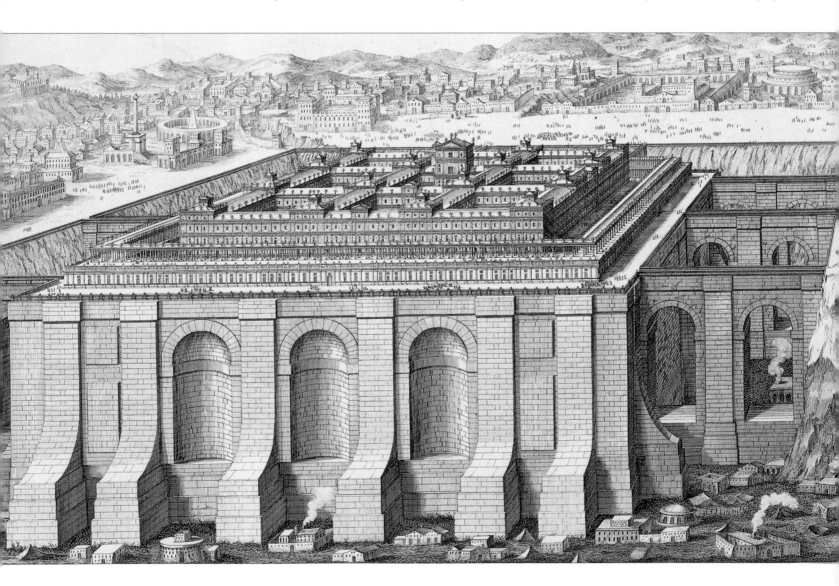

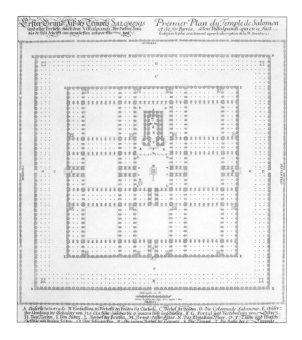

to the second and third storeys. There was no direct access from the side chambers to the temple. The temple itself consisted of an outer hallway, a main sanctuary with an entrance porch framed by two great pillars – opinion is divided as to whether the pillars were freestanding or helping to support the roof – and, separated from the sanctuary by a central open courtyard, an inner *sanctum sanctorum*, or Holy of Holies. Small windows lit the main sanctuary. The walls were covered with cedar panels and the floor with cypress wood, all overlaid with fine gold.

The Holy of Holies was designed as a perfect cube and was windowless. This was where the Ark of the Covenant was kept, along with other tokens of the Israelites' deliverance from captivity in Egypt and of their long journey through the Sinai wilderness. The Ark contained the stone tablets on which were inscribed the Ten Commandments God had given to Moses on Mount Sinai, an "omer of manna" (a specific amount of sacred bread), and the rod of Aaron.

MYTH, LEGEND AND SYMBOL
There was a time when every Masonic writer held unhesitatingly to the belief that Solomon's Temple was where Freemasonry originated – that it was

there that King Solomon, Hiram of Tyre and Hiram Abif presided as Grand Masters over their respective lodges, and the Symbolic Degrees were instituted. Those days are over. Nevertheless, during the long period when hypothesis was accepted as fact, the alleged connection played a decisive part in moulding Masonic ritual and belief.

As a result, almost all the symbolism of Freemasonry rests upon or derives from King Solomon's House of the Lord. Each lodge is a symbol of the temple. Each Worshipful Master represents Solomon himself. Every Freemason is a personification of the temple's builders. The legends that connect Freemasonry with the temple are potent and enduring allegories. Masons now accept them for what their inventors really meant them to be – the foundation stones of a science of morality.

ABOVE LEFT The plan of King Solomon's Temple. The inner sanctuary was quite small, but it was the outer court, terraces and ornate decorations that contributed the most to the temple's legendary splendour.

BELOW God presents the Ten Commandments to Moses in the Wilderness while the Israelites await his return from Mount Sinai. The tablets on which they were written were housed in the temple's innermost sanctum.

EGYPTIAN INFLUENCES

ACCORDING TO MASONIC LEGEND, FREEMASONRY IS AS OLD AS ARCHITECTURE ITSELF. IT IS THEREFORE NOT SURPRISING THAT, IN MASONIC MYTHOLOGY, IT IS HELD THAT THE PROTOTYPES OF INITIATORY ARCHITECTURE WERE EGYPTIAN. ANCIENT EGYPT WAS THE HOME OF HERMETIC MAGIC, DEVELOPED BY THE EGYPTIAN PRIESTS WHO VENERATED THE GOD HERMES TRISMEGISTUS. AS THE MESSENGER OF THE GODS, THE HERALD, THE KEEPER OF MYSTERIES, AND THE GOD OF TRIAL AND INITIATION, THIS GOD WAS AN IMPORTANT FIGURE FOR FREEMASONS. ACCORDINGLY, SPHINXES, PYRAMIDS AND OBELISKS ALL FEATURE PROMINENTLY IN MASONIC ARCHITECTURE AS SYMBOLIC EXPRESSIONS OF MASONIC IDEALS.

BELOW The bringer of wisdom in ancient Egypt, Hermes Trismegistus became associated with Hermetic philosophy in the Middle Ages.

While the late Renaissance Hermetic traditions of Europe had already placed great stock on Egyptian wisdom and religion as an "imperfect harbinger" of Christianity, the Freemasons were to go much further in linking their movement with the Egyptian tradition. The seeds for a modern Egyptian revival were sprouted during the Enlightenment, with its rising curiosity about ancient esoteric religion and allegorical legends. Freemasonry, therefore, helped to bring ancient Egypt into the thinking of the day.

THE FRENCH CONNECTION

Initially, France was the centre of this new interest. The French became fascinated with ancient Egyptian civilization following the invasion of the country by Napoleon in 1798. The First Consul, as he was at that time, took scientists and scholars with him, some of whom

THE FRENCH IN EGYPT

Freemasonry first appeared in Egypt in 1798 when French Masons accompanying Napoleon's invading armies introduced it. Though it has never been established for certain whether Napoleon himself was a Mason – some claim that he was actually initiated in Egypt during the French invasion – four of his brothers held high Masonic offices. Joseph, the eldest, became Grand Master of the Grand Orient of France in 1805. Napoleon certainly tolerated Freemasons and their activities, while the discoveries that were made during his invasion served to consolidate Masonic interest in all things Egyptian.

LEFT Ornately carved and decorated columns line the approaches to the inner regions of the Grand Temple on the island of Philae, one of the great temples of the ancient Egyptians. They worshipped the sun and the sun god. Freemasons seek the inner light and spiritual enlightenment.

BELOW Cleopatra's Needle in New York is an obelisk with a pyramid as its apex. Both were Egyptian architectural inventions and both play important symbolic roles within Freemasonry.

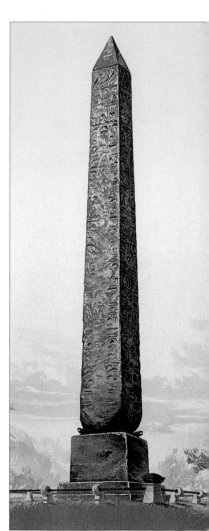

were Masons, and soon they had set to work digging and excavating. Among their discoveries was the Rosetta Stone, which eventually provided the key to the deciphering of hieroglyphs.

As far as French Freemasonry was concerned, the interest in ancient Egypt, which so gripped the public at large as a consequence of the Napoleonic invasion, actually predated that event. Some years before in Paris, the mysterious Count Alessandro Cagliostro had founded the Egyptian Rite of Freemasonry, based upon Egyptian magic and masonry, which attracted many members of the French nobility into its ranks. He also claimed to be an agent of the Order of the Knights Templar and to have received initiation from them on the island of Malta. Today, Cagliostro is almost universally condemned as a charlatan and as an adventurer, but at the time his teachings had considerable impact. According to Manly P. Hall in *Rosicrucian and Masonic Origins*, when the Supreme Council of the Grand Orient called Cagliostro before them to justify his founding of an independent lodge, "they found it difficult to

secure an advocate qualified to discuss with Cagliostro philosophic Masonry and the Ancient Mysteries he claimed to represent".

Though the Egyptian Rite is no longer regarded as a legitimate Masonic ritual, there can be no doubting the impact it had on the Craft at the time and the stimulation it gave to the spread of Egyptian influence. This peaked in the nineteenth century, at a time when Masonic architecture as a whole was becoming more flamboyant and ornate.

In almost every Masonic lodge, there are representations of pyramids and sphinxes. When associated with the Eye of Providence, the pyramid is said to represent the Supreme Being, the Great Architect of the Universe. Another major Masonic symbol that was also important in Egyptian architecture is the obelisk, best described as a tall, vertical tower with a pyramid at its peak. In Freemasonry, obelisks are associated with the sun and various mythologized astronomical phenomena. They are symbols of continuity, power, stability, resurrection and immortality.

CLASSICAL ARCHITECTURE

IN *THE CONSTITUTIONS OF THE FREEMASONS*, ONE OF THE SEMINAL DOCUMENTS OF FREEMASONRY (FIRST PUBLISHED IN 1723), JAMES ANDERSON STATED UNEQUIVOCALLY THAT "THE ARTS OF BUILDING ATTAINED THEIR HIGHEST DEGREE OF PERFECTION UNDER THE ROMAN EMPEROR AUGUSTUS, WHO WAS THE PATRON OF VITRUVIUS". ANDERSON AND HIS FELLOWS EXPECTED MASONS TO SHARE THEIR ENTHUSIASM FOR THE ORDERED ARCHITECTURE OF THE CLASSICAL WORLD AND THEIR DETERMINATION TO USE THE PROCEDURES OF BUILDING TO ILLUSTRATE THE PROCESS OF SPIRITUAL DEVELOPMENT.

The ideas put forward by Marcus Vitruvius Pollio – to give the great Roman architect and engineer his full name – in his *De Architectura Libri Decem* (Ten Books on Architecture) were themselves encapsulations of the best and most important precepts of the classical architectural tradition. According to Masonic tradition, these precepts derived from the Temple of Solomon. Pythagoras brought the secrets of architecture, which were carved on the two pillars of the temple that play such important symbolic roles in Masonic ritual, back to Greece, from where they spread to the West. They were centred on the two cardinal ideals of order and simplicity. The Masons revere three of the classical architectural orders: Corinthian, Doric and Ionic. In Masonic architectural symbolism, Doric stands for strength, Ionic for wisdom and Corinthian for beauty.

ABOVE An architectural representation of a classic pillar design. According to Masonic tradition, classical architecture derived its most important principles from King Solomon's Temple where Freemasonry was born.

RIGHT The five classical Orders of Architecture: from left to right, Tuscan, Doric, Ionian, Corinthian and Composite. Three of them – Corinthian, Doric, and Ionian – feature in Masonic architectural symbolism.

BUILDING A TRADITION

Masonic thinking was also influenced by the Renaissance concept of the architect as the Universal Man, master of all the arts central to human knowledge. From the eighteenth century onwards, initiates could receive instruction in mathematics and listen to lectures on the new science at Masonic lodges. They became part of a fellowship that claimed to be descended from the earliest Masonic architects who constructed the ancient temples, and those who designed the medieval cathedrals and practised the "Royal Art". One such eighteenth-century paragon was Batty Langley, a Freemason and an architect, who ran a building school in London. According to the prospectus, Langley taught "young Noblemen and Gentlemen to draw the Orders of Columns in

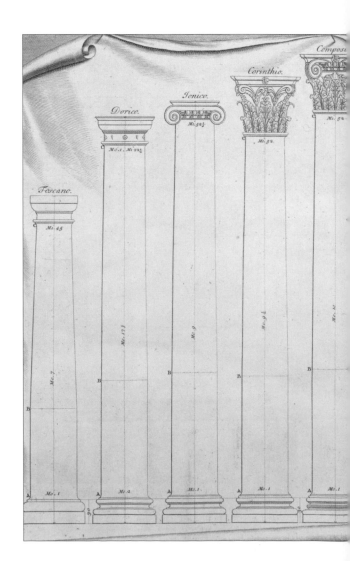

Architecture, to design Geometrical Plans and Elevations for Temples, Hermitages, Caves, Grottoes, Cascades, Theatres, and other Ornamental Buildings of Delight, to lay out and improve Parks and Gardens".

Possibly unconsciously, Langley was following one of Vitruvius' cardinal precepts. In *The Education of an Architect*, Vitruvius wrote that an architect "should be equipped with knowledge of many branches of study and varied kinds of learning, for it is by his judgement that all work done by the other arts is put to the test".

This was a view with which Freemasonry was quick to concur. The Craft approved wholeheartedly of the dominant Palladian style, which, taking its cue from the neo-classical work of the Italian architect Palladio, demanded that every great building conform to the orders of architecture that had been prescribed by the ancient Greeks. That legacy persists. In the rituals that accompany admission to the

Fellow Craft Degree, for instance, architecture features prominently, with elaborate descriptions and assessments of the importance of each of the classical orders.

ABOVE Frontispiece of an architectural study printed in Renaissance Venice. According to Renaissance thinking, architects were masters of all the arts central to knowledge. The parallel with Freemasonry and its beliefs is obvious.

ABOVE LEFT The column supporting the elaborate pediment in this drawing, signed by Batty and Thomas Langley, is Corinthian – a Masonic symbol of beauty.

LEFT Italian architect Andrea Palladio was the leader of the classical revival and, as such, was later revered by the new generation of Speculative Freemasons in the eighteenth century.

MASONIC BUILDINGS

LODGES AND TEMPLES HAVE NOT ALWAYS BEEN IMPOSING WORKS OF ARCHITECTURE. IN THE EARLY DAYS, FEW MASONIC LODGES HAD PREMISES OF THEIR OWN — THEY MET IN THE UPSTAIRS ROOMS OF TAVERNS AND COFFEE HOUSES. EVEN THE PREMIER GRAND LODGE OF ENGLAND DID NOT POSSESS A PERMANENT HOME UNTIL 1775 WHEN A HOUSE WAS PURCHASED IN GREAT QUEEN STREET.

BELOW Freemason's Tavern, Lincoln's Inn Fields, London, hosted the inaugural dinner of the Royal Astronomical Society in 1820. The event is clear evidence of Freemasonry's continuing links with speculative science.

The architecture of the lodge is particularly important for imparting the appropriate solemnity during Masonic ceremonies. There is also a commonality to the style of Masonic architecture, wherever it is found, and it exists in a time warp of its own devising. If a Mason of today could travel back in time to an eighteenth-century lodge, he would find many architectural similarities.

Masonic buildings are sometimes called temples, because much of the symbolism that Freemasonry uses to teach its lessons comes from the building of the Temple of King Solomon in the Holy Land. The term lodge comes from the structures that medieval Masons built against the sides of cathedrals during their construction. In winter, when work on the building had to stop, they lived in these lodges and worked at carving stone.

However, perhaps the most significant feature is the layout of the lodge itself. According to Masonic lore, this should ideally follow the supposed layout of King Solomon's Temple as

closely as possible. It should have a porch with two pillars, a main sanctuary and an inner Holy of Holies. The two pillars, Jachin and Boaz, have in themselves considerable symbolic importance in Masonic ritual.

BACK TO THE EGYPTIANS

There was a further predominant influence on the architecture of lodge buildings – that of ancient Egypt. From the nineteenth century onwards, it became the norm for Masons to incorporate elements of Egyptian design into their buildings, just as Egyptian thought came to play a significant part in actual Masonic ritual. The 31st Degree of the Scottish Rite, as devised by noted nineteenth-century Masonic scholar Albert Pike, was based on the Book of the Dead (a record of ancient Egyptian mortuary spells) and includes references to the murder of the god Osiris and his resurrection.

The large windowless lodge room of the Silvergate Temple in San Diego, California, for example, was designed to be an exact replica of an Egyptian throne room, while in the Royal Arch Halls of the Chapter Room, Edinburgh, the use of Egyptian motifs extended to the furniture and carpets. The George Washington Masonic National Memorial in Virginia is a replica of the mighty Pharos of Alexandria, one of the original Seven Wonders of the Ancient World.

THE GRANDEST TEMPLE

The Masonic Temple in Detroit, which was dedicated in 1926, is still the largest and most complex building of its kind in the world. The 14-storey tower is Gothic in inspiration. There are seven Craft Lodge Rooms – all have different decorative treatments, inspired by Egyptian, Doric, Ionic, Corinthian, Italian Renaissance, Byzantine, Gothic and Romanesque motifs. The rooms are all faithful to the period.

ABOVE The Pharos of Alexandria was the inspiration for George Washington's Masonic Memorial in Virginia.

ABOVE LEFT Building the first pyramid at Giza. The use of skilled stonemakers could be interpreted as evidence of a link with the beginnings of Freemasonry.

BELOW A nineteenth-century French Master Mason's Apron. The main symbolic theme is architectural imagery.

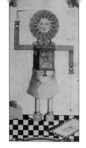

THE LODGE INTERIOR

IN COMMON WITH OTHER RITUALISTIC SOCIETIES, FREEMASONRY PLACES ENORMOUS IMPORTANCE ON THE ARRANGEMENTS OF ITS MEETING PLACES. TO MASONS, THE LODGE REFERS BOTH TO A MEETING OF A GROUP OF MASONS AND TO THE ROOM OR BUILDING IN WHICH THE GATHERING TAKES PLACE. ONLY WHEN PURPOSE-BUILT LODGES AND TEMPLES BECAME THE NORM WERE MASONS ABLE TO SET OUT THEIR FURNITURE AND EQUIPMENT ON A MORE OR LESS PERMANENT BASIS, AND THE LAYOUT ITSELF BECAME AN IMPORTANT AND CONSTANT MASONIC SYMBOL.

BELOW A grand dinner in Freemason's Hall, London. The scene is an eloquent testament to the way Freemasonry has grown since the days of meetings in hired rooms above taverns and coffee houses.

Lodges conventionally take the form of oblong squares, though records show that some early ones seem to have been triangular and others cruciform. Generally, as far as Blue Lodge Freemasonry is concerned, the traditional English floor plan is followed. The Worshipful Master of the Lodge sits in the east, which Masonic lore associates with the sun, light and life. At the other end of the lodge are three steps, one for the First Degree, one for the Second Degree and one for the Third. There is always an altar or table with the Volume of Sacred Law open on it if a lodge is meeting.

Because Masons consider protecting the secrets of their ceremonies to be so important, lodges usually lack windows. Instead, they are lit by candlelight. The candles themselves have their own

significance as symbols of spiritual light or illumination. They are also associated with the notions of consecration, gratitude and the keeping of promises.

LODGE FURNISHINGS

The first lodges probably had simple decor, but as the Craft began to attract new adherents and Freemasonry grew in power, wealth and prestige, so decoration and furnishing grew to be more elaborate. Intricate floor cloths, for instance, became the norm – typical examples showed the two pillars Boaz and Jachin, the seven steps that tradition had it led to Solomon's Temple, the temple's Mosaic Pavement, the Flaming Star, the Sun, the Perpendicular and other significant Masonic emblems.

Other features worthy of comment include the All-Seeing Eye – a perpetual symbol signifying the omnipresence and omniscience of the Supreme Being – the Blazing Star and the Signs of the Zodiac. With the exception of white, blue is the only colour used in Masonic decoration; it symbolizes universal friendship and benevolence.

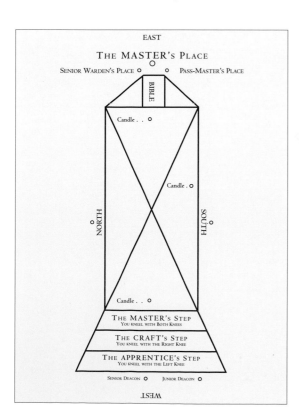

Freemasons revere King Solomon's Temple as a symbol of what has been lost and as an inspiration for what could be reconstructed through the enlightened pursuit of strength, wisdom and beauty. This was the foundation they built on to create a mystic symbolism that was uniquely their own. Take the chequered floor to be found in many Masonic lodges as an example. To the outsider, it is a floor – nothing more, nothing less. To the Freemason, its multiplicity of squares is far more than simply attractive decoration. They symbolize among other things, the chequered life of the unenlightened man.

The chairs in which the Master of the Lodge and other lodge officers sit are the most dramatic group of furnishings found in the lodge. Many are in a style that can be termed architectonic, for they are as much pieces of architecture as they are furniture. They are a microcosm of overall lodge design, featuring columns, roofs and cornices as part of their decoration, while their long, solidly formulated arms suggest parallel lines.

ABOVE A Freemason "torged through the tools of his Lodge" as depicted in a 1754 English illustration. The architectural links are clearly visible.

FAR LEFT A plan of a typical Masonic lodge. Note where the lodge officers sit, and the three steps – one for each of the Three Degrees.

A UNIVERSAL SYMBOL

The Square and Compasses design is known throughout the world as a symbol of character, charity and brotherly love. This particular emblem features prominently in the decoration of the Masonic lodge.

GARDENS

COINCIDING WITH THE RISE OF SPECULATIVE FREEMASONRY IN ENGLAND CAME THE BIRTH OF THE LANDSCAPE GARDEN. JUST AS THE VITRUVIAN CONCEPT OF ARCHITECTURE AS THE CULMINATION OF ALL OTHER STUDIES BECAME A FUNDAMENTAL TENET OF ENLIGHTENMENT FREEMASONRY, SO TOO DID THE NOTION OF GARDEN DESIGN AS A FURTHER EXPRESSION OF MASONIC PRINCIPLES. MANY OF THE FOREMOST GARDEN DESIGNERS OF THE DAY WERE FREEMASONS, SO IT IS NOT SURPRISING THAT THEY UTILIZED A VAST VOCABULARY OF MASONIC SYMBOLS IN THEIR CREATIONS.

BELOW The garden chapel at Strawberry Hill, England, home of the eighteenth-century writer and wit Horace Walpole. The idyll he created reflected the Masonic idea of order, morality, virtue, fraternity and tolerance.

Enthusiasm for the new art of gardening was not confined to England – it spread to France, Germany and other parts of Europe, just as the ideas and ideals of Freemasonry itself were disseminated. In Europe as in England, the new gardens were deliberately intended to evoke the ideal of uncorrupted Elysium. Such gardens, it was felt, could play their part in bringing about a new golden age of increasing social harmony and perfection. This was a prime Masonic ambition. The idea was to shape the landscape to expound an explicit moral lesson.

LANDSCAPE ARCHITECTURE

For Masonic garden designers, architecture and garden ornament were just as important as the planning of the garden itself – indeed, the two were inseparable. Again, the links with Freemasonry and Masonic symbolism are specific. Great "gardens of allusion", as they came to be known, were created at Castle Howard in Yorkshire, England; Strawberry Hill, home of Horace Walpole, near London, England; Stowe; and at the philosopher Jean-Jacques Rousseau's home in Ermenonville, France. The author of *Le Contrat Social* is buried on an island in the grounds.

Circular rotundas began to feature in garden architecture. These temple-like buildings had various Masonic and allegorical properties attributed to them. Sphinxes made their appearance, along with pyramids, obelisks and other features influenced by the Egyptians. These were also an expression of Masonic traditions, notably the notion of a direct link between the Craft and the ancient Egyptian Mysteries.

LEFT Sir John Vanbrugh, Charles Bridgeman, William Kent and James Gibbs all contributed to the creation of Stowe's great "garden of allusion". The rotunda was undoubtedly inspired by Freemasonry.

BELOW Lilies have long been associated with Freemasonry – the capitals of the two pillars of King Solomon's Temple were decorated with them. The rotunda in the background is also Masonic in inspiration.

Nicholas Hawksmoor, William Kent and Sir John Vanbrugh, three celebrated garden designers of the early eighteenth century, were noted for their employment of pyramids. Kent, for instance, placed a stepped pyramid over the central block of the Temple of British Worthies he erected at Stowe, setting a bust of Mercury within its oval niche. Mercury was an important figure in Masonic legend. His earlier name had been Hermes Trismegistus and he was linked with Euclid, Pythagoras and the supposed Egyptian foundations of the Craft.

GOETHE AND GARDENS

The German poet Johann Wolfgang von Goethe was a prominent Freemason who made the creation of a new garden and its buildings along Masonic lines a major theme in one of his novels, *Die Wahlverwandtschaften*. The text has plenty of Masonic imagery, with references to "square-cut stones", a symbol of order and regularity, and the "lime mortar" in which these stones are to be embedded. Lime mortar was important in Goethe's day because of its "binding force". The parallel, as Goethe pointed out, is the way in which law acts as social cement within human society.

FUNERARY GARDENS
So-called funerary gardens began to be designed along the same lines. Probably the grandest and most influential of them all is the great cemetery of Père-Lachaise, Paris, created by French Mason Alexandre-Théodore Brongniart and opened in 1804. In the cemetery, dignified classical tombs lined the avenues, each of which had its own distinctive planting of limes, chestnuts, poplars and, above all, acacias. The acacia has long been esteemed as a sacred tree and acacias are extremely important in Masonic context. Not only did the plant have historic Egyptian associations, but, according to Masonic tradition, a sprig of it had been planted as a marker for Hiram Abif's grave. In Masonic symbolism, it is a token of the immortality of the soul.

PART FOUR

SIGNS AND SYMBOLS

 Early historical evidence for the origins of Freemasonry is very meagre. However, we do know that the originators of modern Freemasonry were people who wanted to build a better world in which men could work peacefully together for the good of mankind. As was the custom they used allegory and symbolism to pass on their ideals. Since their central tenet was based on building, they took their chief allegory from the Bible, and it is from the Bible that many signs and symbols are derived. History, mythology and classical legend feature too, and a great deal of the symbolism is mathematical and geometrical in nature. Freemasonry does not impose meanings on its symbols, although many have gained a general acceptance as to what they represent.

RIGHT Jacob dreams of a ladder or stairway from Earth to Heaven as related in Genesis, the first book of the Bible. The ladder is an important symbol in Freemasonry.

THE WORKING TOOLS

FREEMASONRY'S SO-CALLED WORKING TOOLS ARE THE COMPASSES, THE SQUARE, THE 24-INCH GAUGE, THE GAVEL, THE PLUMB, THE LEVEL AND THE TROWEL. IN OPERATIVE FREEMASONRY THESE WERE THE TOOLS OF THE STONEMASON'S TRADE. IN SPECULATIVE FREEMASONRY THEY TOOK ON A SYMBOLIC MEANING; SPECIFIC VIRTUES AND PRINCIPLES WERE ASSIGNED TO EACH WORKING TOOL. OF THEM, THE SQUARE AND COMPASSES ARE PROBABLY THE MOST SIGNIFICANT, AND CERTAINLY THE BEST KNOWN.

ABOVE The seal or stamp of the Grand Lodge of Ireland depicts a Trowel, the principal working tool of a Master Mason.

BELOW Each Working Tool of Freemasonry has its own importance. Collectively, they have been dubbed "the evangelists of a new day".

THE SQUARE AND COMPASSES

Two of the Three Great Lights of Freemasonry are the Square and Compasses and thus they have major parts to play in the Masonic rituals associated with initiation into the Three Degrees. In the First Degree, the Square is one of the three Great Lights; in the Second, it is a Working Tool; and in the Third it is the emblem of the Master of the Lodge. How it is depicted differs. French Freemasons almost invariably show it with one leg longer than the other, but in American Freemasonry it has legs of equal length. Regardless of this, its symbolic meaning is constant. It stands for morality, honesty and fair dealing.

The Compasses are Freemasonry's most prominent symbol of truth and loyalty. It is believed that while the Volume of Sacred Law sheds light on a Mason's duty to the Supreme Being, and the Square illustrates the duty he owes to his fellow Masons and to society, so the Compasses provide the extra light necessary to understand the duties he owes himself – to circumscribe passions and keep desires within bounds. Some Masons believe that the Compasses are a symbol of the sun, the circular pivot representing the sun's body and the diverging legs its rays.

OTHER WORKING TOOLS

The 24-inch Gauge is a two-foot-long rule, which is subdivided into one-inch dimensions. In the First Degree, these divisions represent the hours of the day and their purpose is to teach Entered Apprentices the necessity of devoting their time to good purpose.

The Common Gavel, or stonemason's hammer, is similarly one of the Entered Apprentice's important Working Tools. Operative Masons used

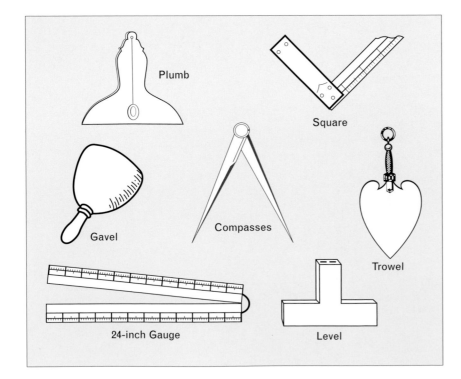

Plumb

Square

Gavel

Compasses

Trowel

24-inch Gauge

Level

SYMBOLIC MEANINGS

The Square and the Compasses are the best known tools in Freemasonry. The Square stands for morality, honesty and fair dealing, and the Compasses symbolize truth and loyalty.

Gavels to break off the corners of Rough Ashlars to make the stones ready for use in building. In Speculative Freemasonry, the Gavel stands as a reminder of the necessity of divesting heart and conscience of what are termed the vices and superfluities of life. The Gavel used by the Master of a lodge is also called a Hiram, because – like the architect – it governs the Craft and keeps order in the lodge as Hiram did in King Solomon's Temple.

The Trowel is the tool used by Operative Masons for the physical process of spreading building cement. In Speculative Freemasonry it symbolizes "the noble and glorious purpose of spreading the cement of brotherly love and affection". It is the Working Tool of a Third Degree Master Mason, where it is considered to cement and complete the work of the previous two degrees.

ABOVE Architectural emblems on this Masonic medal symbolize the various qualities that make up truth.

RIGHT A Junior Grand Warden's Jewel of Office depicts the Plumb, which together with the Level is a symbol of the Fellow Craft Degree.

ABOVE The Master of an Irish Lodge in 1787 is portrayed sitting between two columns symbolizing the twin pillars of King Solomon's Temple. Items on the altar include the Bible and a collection of Working Tools.

THE SYMBOLIC TEMPLE

THE TEMPLE IS A PRE-EMINENT MASONIC SYMBOL, SIGNIFYING "THAT HOUSE NOT MADE WITH HANDS, ETERNAL IN THE HEAVENS". IT IS AN EMBLEM OF HOPE FOR THE FUTURE. THE LINKS BETWEEN KING SOLOMON'S TEMPLE AND THE PRACTICE OF THE ART CERTAINLY DATE BACK TO THE DAYS OF OPERATIVE MASONRY, WHEN CANDIDATES IN EACH OF ITS SEVERAL DEGREES WERE TAUGHT THAT THEY REPRESENTED A PARTICULAR STONE REQUIRED IN THE CONSTRUCTION OF THE GREAT EDIFICE. THE SUBSEQUENT CEREMONIES WERE WOVEN AROUND THE PREPARING, TESTING AND POSITIONING OF THAT STONE IN PLACE.

BELOW The Temple of Solomon depicted by an eighteenth-century artist. Whether Solomon was a Mason or not, there is no doubting his Temple's continued importance as a powerful and enduring allegorical symbol.

Biblical records leave no doubt that Masons and associated craftsmen working together on the construction of King Solomon's Temple must have had comprehensive knowledge of the symbolism of the building they were creating. Every single feature of the great building was of religious and symbolic significance. Even after the Temple's destruction by Nebuchadnezzar II, its continuing importance was recognized in the building of the

Second Temple and its subsequent restoration. Flavius Josephus, the Roman Governor of Galilee centuries later, recorded in his *Antiquities of the Jews* (AD93) that when King Herod the Great began building work on the Second Temple in 20BC he not only carried it out piecemeal to avoid interrupting the ritual observances, but he also had a thousand priests trained to work as Masons in rebuilding the shrine.

SYMBOLS AND ALLEGORIES

In Freemasonry all Masonic lodges and temples are held to be symbolic representations of King Solomon's Temple. The so-called perambulations of candidates around the lodge during the initiation process to the various Masonic Degrees are closely linked to the original temple rituals. A wide range of Working Tools of the Craft are used to provide moral instruction, which contains frequent references to work on the temple.

According to John Hamill in *The Craft: A History of English Freemasonry*, as an initiate passes through the various ceremonies he learns that the skilled Masons employed to build the temple were divided into Apprentices and Fellows, presided

THE TEMPLE'S LEGACY

Although built in 967BC to stand for centuries, the Temple was destroyed within a few hundred years. Its influence has been incalculable.

over by three Grand Masters – Solomon himself, King Hiram of Tyre and Hiram Abif – who kept certain secrets of the Craft known only to them. These secrets were lost as a result of Hiram Abif's murder, after which substitute secrets were adopted "until time or circumstance should restore the former". Obviously, despite the implication that Freemasonry was already established in Solomon's time, the ritual is not historically true. It is a dramatic allegory through which the tenets of the Craft are passed on from one generation of Masons to the next. Another such allegory is that of the great cornerstone, or keystone, required to complete the arch of the secret vault.

Specific features of King Solomon's Temple, such as the two great pillars that stood at its entrance, are also used as Masonic symbols. These columns are Freemasonry's closest physical link to the original temple and they have featured in Masonic ritual right up to the present day.

ABOVE King Solomon built a great temple in Jerusalem, and in doing so fulfilled the dreams of his father, David.

BELOW By the time Jerusalem was burned by the Romans in AD70, the original temple of Solomon had long since vanished, and the Second Temple, built by Herod, was in its place.

THE GREAT PYRAMID

AS FAR AS ITS RITUALS ARE CONCERNED, MODERN FREEMASONRY HAS CERTAINLY BEEN INFLUENCED BY ANCIENT EGYPTIAN BELIEFS. THOUGH THERE IS NO HARD HISTORICAL EVIDENCE TO SUPPORT THIS, ACCORDING TO MYTHOLOGY THE FOUNDATIONS OF THE MASONIC BROTHERHOOD DATE BACK TO THE ORIGINS OF ARCHITECTURE ITSELF. HENCE, SO IT IS ARGUED, THERE MUST BE A LINK BETWEEN MASONRY AND THE PYRAMIDS, THE OLDEST EXAMPLES OF MONUMENTAL ARCHITECTURE TO SURVIVE.

BELOW The pyramids are depicted with the Sphinx in the foreground. From the late eighteenth century onwards, Freemasons were dedicated Egyptophiles and pyramids therefore came to feature in their symbolism.

Some scholars believe that the spiritual doctrines embodied within Masonic ritual are extremely ancient, influenced by the teachings of many faiths and philosophies since time immemorial. Foremost among those influences was the religion of ancient Egypt, the oldest written records of which survive in the so-called *Pyramid Texts* – the hieroglyphic inscriptions on three pyramids in the vicinity of Saqqara. The texts revolve around the notion of a circle of existence, which the Egyptians themselves believed was represented by progress through the various chambers in the

Great Pyramid. The idea of a ritual journey was later to appear in ancient Greek and other cultures. The Greek architect Daedalus, the supposed inventor of the axe, awl and bevel, designed and built the great labyrinth at Knossos, in Crete – the world's first maze.

The similarities between such rituals and Masonic rites are evident. The ceremonies in modern Speculative Freemasonry include the symbolic elements of the circle of existence. According to Maurizio Nicosia in *The Sepulchre of Osiris*, "the rite is organized as a pyramid…

Some say that Ptah himself was the resurrection of Osiris, who also plays a significant part in Masonic myth and legend.

Imhotep himself was to become a god – the divine son in the Triad of Memphis. Little is known about Imhotep's architectural precepts other than his over-riding belief that, above all, a building needs firm, lasting foundations: he held that columns and pillars were the best means of providing the necessary stability. Later, worship of Imhotep became widespread in the Graeco-Roman world.

LEFT A Masonic medal shows clear Egyptian influences. Some claim that the decision to feature a pyramid and All-Seeing Eye on the US Great Seal was Masonically inspired.

BELOW The passage from the Second to the Third Gallery in the Great Pyramid. Just like the Masons, the Egyptians believed in the idea of a ritual journey, which these passageways represent.

the pyramid image immediately leads to the Egyptian sepulchres and to the journey of detachment from the body and rising, which constitute the target of the initiation".

THE FIRST ARCHITECT

Another reason for the close association of Freemasons with pyramids is that the very first one was planned and built by the world's first known architect. This is the stepped pyramid, which was also erected at Saqqara. The man was Imhotep, chief architect to King Zoser; according to Egyptian mythology he was the son of the god Ptah, god of fire and the architect of the universe.

THE EGYPTIAN LEGACY

From the late eighteenth century, all manner of secret societies and cults – from the Rosicrucians to the Freemasons – were quick to seize on the trappings of the culture and religion of ancient Egypt. Their idea was to confer a kind of instant antiquity on their rites and practices; in some cases, they went as far as to claim direct succession from the Egyptian priesthood itself. Freemasons, in particular, saw their lodges as Egyptian temples and decorated them accordingly with all manner of Egyptian symbols – notably hieroglyphs. What is clear, however, is that although the pyramid is a Masonic symbol, it is only one of many Egyptian influences.

SOLOMON'S COLUMNS

In Freemasonry today, the most significant pillars are the huge twin columns that originally stood in the porchway of King Solomon's Temple in Jerusalem. The column to the left, named Boaz, was carved with the phrase "May the Lord establish the throne of David and his kingdom for his seed forever." The column to the right was named Jachin, and its inscription read "In the strength of the Lord shall the king rejoice."

ABOVE The Hathor Column at Dendera in Egypt. The huge pillars undoubtedly had much the same symbolic significance as those of King Solomon's Temple.

However, Boaz and Jachin were not the first columns to feature in Masonic lore. As recorded in the Old Charges, the children of Lamech made the two earliest pillars in the story of the Craft in readiness for the destruction of the world by fire or flood. The pillars were indestructible, and so on them were carved details of "all the sciences" that had been discovered up to that time to ensure that knowledge survived the disaster.

SYMBOLISM OF BOAZ AND JACHIN
These twin columns are almost as familiar symbols of Freemasonry as the Square and Compasses. In Masonic ritual, Boaz and Jachin symbolize among other things wisdom and understanding, and their respective symbolic significances are explained as part of the rites surrounding admission to the First and Second Degrees. They made their first recorded appearance in Craft ritual in 1696 in Scotland, though it appears likely that they had already achieved an important place in it some time between 1500 and 1630. Soon after this, the pillars became a regular part of the furnishings of the lodge.

DEVELOPMENT OF THE COLUMNS
At the start, the twin pillars were drawn on the floor in chalk and charcoal with the Lesser Lights – three candles representing "the sun to rule the day, the moon, the night, and Master

Mason his lodge" – arranged in a triangle to illuminate them. By the mid-eighteenth century, however, it is clear that the Lodge Wardens possessed their own versions. According to *Three Distinct Knocks*, a pamphlet purporting to expose Masonic proceedings published in 1768, "the Senior and Junior Wardens have each of their Columns in their Hand, about Twenty

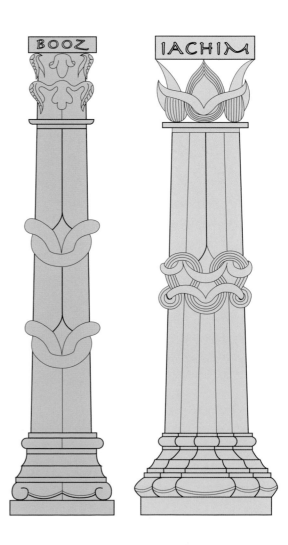

Inches long, which represent the two Columns of the Porch at Solomon's Temple. Boaz and Jachin. The Senior is Boaz or Strength. The Junior is Jachin or Wisdom."

Finally, the two columns appeared as handsome pieces of furniture surmounted with brass bowls or globes covered with celestial and terrestrial maps and usually standing at the western end of the lodge. In this position they form a portal, and candidates for initiation into the Three Degrees pass between them.

Pillars and columns also feature prominently in Masonic architecture. Single columns often serve as memorials, while twin pillars suggest stability and imply strength. Groups of three pillars suggest cooperation and imply perfection. Groups of four represent earth, water, air and fire, to suggest completeness and imply fulfilment.

LEFT Pillars supporting globes decorated with celestial and terrestrial maps feature prominently on some Masonic tracing boards as part of King Solomon's Temple.

BELOW A fifteenth-century view of the walled city of Jerusalem showing the Temple of Solomon and the city gates, taken from the Nuremberg Chronicle.

OPPOSITE The pillars of Boaz and Jachin have allegorical significance in Masonic symbolism. Boaz means "in strength"; the right pillar Jachin means "for God will establish", a reminder of the abundant promises of God.

EARLY PILLARS

Part of the Cooke Manuscript describes the two earliest pillars in Freemasonry as being created by the children of Lamech. The first known mention of Solomon's pillars in Craft ritual is found in a Scottish manuscript (from 1696) in a catechism associated with the "Mason Word" ceremonies. When Masonic ceremonies were reshaped to include an allegorical link to King Solomon's Temple, the Temple pillars were substituted for the earlier ones.

THE ALL-SEEING EYE

THE EYE OF PROVIDENCE, AS THE ALL-SEEING EYE IS OFTEN TERMED, IS A SYMBOL SHOWING AN EYE SURROUNDED BY RAYS OF LIGHT, OR A GLORY, AND USUALLY ENCLOSED BY A TRIANGLE. IT IS COMMONLY INTERPRETED AS REPRESENTING THE EYE OF GOD — IN MASONIC PARLANCE, THE SUPREME BEING — KEEPING A WATCH OVER MANKIND. ITS ORIGINS CAN BE TRACED BACK TO ANCIENT EGYPTIAN MYTHOLOGY AND THE EYE OF HORUS. FOR THE EGYPTIANS, THIS WAS A SYMBOL OF POWER AND PROTECTION.

BELOW The Eye of Providence and the G (Great Architect) looks down benevolently on the Masonic progress towards enlightenment.

In Freemasonry, the All-Seeing Eye serves as a reminder to Masons that the Great Architect of the Universe always observes their deeds. Typically, it has a semicircular glory below the actual eye, the lowest rays often extending farther down. Sometimes it is enclosed within a triangle, which is perhaps a reference to the Masonic preference for the number three in numerology. In other variations, the letter G, standing for the Great Architect, replaces the eye itself.

THE ORIGINAL ALL-SEEING EYE

In Masonic literature, the first historical reference to the All-Seeing Eye appears to have been in Thomas Smith Webb's *The Freemasons Monitor*, published in 1797. In this title, Smith Webb wrote that "although our thoughts, words and actions may be hidden from the eyes of man, yet the All-Seeing Eye, whom the Sun, Moon and Stars obey, and under whose watchful care even Comets perform their stupendous revolutions, pervades the innermost recesses of the human heart and will reward us according to our merits".

Webb's book appeared well over a decade after the Eye of Providence was adopted as part of the symbolism on the reverse side of the Great Seal of the United States. On the seal, it is surrounded by the words *annuit coeptis*, which, roughly translated, mean "it is favourable to our undertakings". The Eye of Providence is positioned above an unfinished pyramid whose 13 steps represent the original 13 states and that anticipates the future growth of the nation. Taken together, the implication is that the Eye — or God — favours American prosperity.

FAR LEFT A pyramid and the Eye feature on the dollar bill (Great Seal). Despite what anti-Masonic writers say, there is no evidence that Freemasonry inspired their presence.

LEFT The Eye of God watches over humanity. The symbol is not unique to Freemasonry; it often features in Christian art.

BELOW An elaborate invitation to Lodge meetings features the All-Seeing Eye, the Sun, the Moon and the two pillars of King Solomon's Temple. All are Masonic symbols.

Given the active and constant anti-Masonic propaganda, it seems highly unlikely that Freemasonry had anything to do with the Great Seal's origins. None of the designers of the Seal was a Mason. It seems likely that the misinterpretation of the Great Seal as a Masonic symbol started in 1884, when Eliot Charles Norton, a Harvard professor, wrote that the reverse "can hardly look otherwise than as a dull emblem of a Masonic fraternity". From that seemingly innocuous comment, an elaborate Masonic conspiracy theory grew, which is still accepted by many even today.

In fact, although Freemasonry may have eventually adopted the notion of the All-Seeing Eye, it is not a uniquely Masonic symbol at all. The eye inside an equilateral triangle, point up or point down, often appears in Christian art, while the depiction of a single eye was a well-established artistic convention for an "omniscient ubiquitous deity" in Renaissance times.

EYE OF HORUS

Known as the *indjat* or *wedjet* by the ancient Egyptians, the Eye of Horus was the symbol of the falcon-headed god Horus and Re, the Sun god. It was said to have healing and protective powers. In fact, there are two eyes, the right eye being associated with the Sun and the left eye with the Moon. The two eyes represent the balance between reason and intuition and light and dark.

SUN AND BLAZING STAR

IN FREEMASONRY, THE SUN AND THE MOON TOGETHER REPRESENT WISDOM, POWER AND GOODNESS, WHILE THE BLAZING STAR IS AN EMBLEM OF DIVINITY AND OF RESURRECTION. THIS IS NOT SURPRISING, SINCE ONE OF THE CHIEF AIMS OF THE CRAFT IS TO GUIDE ITS INITIATES ALONG THE PATH THAT LEADS TO THE TRUE LIGHT. HOWEVER, REFERENCES IN MASONIC WRITINGS TO THESE AND OTHER ASTRONOMICAL PHENOMENA HAVE LED MANY TO BELIEVE THAT FREEMASONRY IS LINKED TO ASTROLOGY THROUGH ITS HISTORY, BELIEFS AND PRACTICES. NOTHING COULD BE FURTHER FROM THE TRUTH.

RIGHT The earth, sun and moon feature on this Masonic medal.

FAR RIGHT Another Masonic medal highlights the Blazing Star.

BELOW A seventeenth-century astronomer. The study of the stars is an important feature of Freemasonry.

THE SUN

Ways of linking Freemasonry to the ancient and arcane rituals of sun worship started some time in the nineteenth century and have persisted up to the present day.

In their 1977 book *The Hiram Key* for instance, Christopher Knight and Robert Lomas state: "Freemasons today claim always to meet symbolically at noon on the basis that Freemasonry is a worldwide organization and therefore the Sun is always at its meridian with respect to Freemasonry. Masonic reference to God as 'the most high' is therefore a description of Re, the sun god of the ancient Egyptians, in his ultimate position, the zenith of the heavens at noon." By the same token, attempts have been made to prove that some of the mystical words in Masonic ritual are "pure Egyptian". If anything, however, the origins of such words can be traced back to ancient Hebrew.

None the less, it is the case that there are links between the Craft and astronomy. As early as AD819, the Archbishop of Mainz wrote: "Astronomy teaches the laws of the stellar world, which is built up on the investigation of natural phenomena in order to determine the course of the sun, the moon, and the stars and to effect a proper reckoning of time." This is very close to what Masons believe.

THE BLAZING STAR

Similarly, anti-Masonic writers have made attempts to link the Blazing Star of Freemasonry with the worship of Venus and participation in occult rituals. This, too, is incorrect. Along with the Mosaic Pavement and Indented Tessel, the Blazing Star is one of the Ornaments of the Lodge and features briefly in the rituals that accompany admission to the First Degree.

The Blazing Star has a double symbolism, similar to that of the Indented Tessel, which is the border or skirting that surrounds the pavement. The first is straightforward – the star symbolizes the sun – but is of secondary importance. The star's prime purpose is to symbolize the Supreme Being, reminding us of "the omnipresence of the Almighty" and the fact that "wherever we may be assembled together, God is in the midst of us,

seeing our actions and observing the secret intents and desires of our hearts". The star is identified with the Star of Bethlehem that alerted the shepherds to the birth of Jesus and guided the Three Wise Men across the desert to the scene.

MASONS AND THE SUN

The sun is one of the Lesser Lights of Freemasonry. As a source of light, it is a reminder to Masons to strive for intellectual enlightenment. This is one of the reasons why all ceremonies in Freemasons' lodges are performed facing east. Masonic ritual proclaims that "as the sun rises in the east to open and govern the day, so rises the Worshipful Master in the east to open and govern his Lodge". Together with the moon, which governs and rules the night, the sun represents the active forces of nature, which must be in balance for the latter to exist.

ABOVE According to Masonic ritual, an understanding of the "laws of the stellar world" is vital "to effect a proper reckoning of time".

BELOW An Irish Masonic jewel from the late eighteenth century features the Blazing Star and other symbols.

THE MOON

IN MODERN MASONIC RITUAL, THE MOON IS THE SECOND OF THE LESSER LIGHTS OF FREEMASONRY. ITS PLACE IN THE MASONIC PANTHEON STEMS FIRST FROM THE BOOK OF GENESIS, IN WHICH IT IS RELATED HOW, ON THE FOURTH DAY OF CREATION, GOD "MADE TWO GREAT LIGHTS; THE GREATER LIGHT TO RULE THE DAY AND THE LESSER LIGHT TO RULE THE NIGHT". IT IS ALSO LINKED TO THE PRACTICE OF ALCHEMY IN MEDIEVAL TIMES, FOR IT WAS THE ALCHEMISTS WHO FIRST GAVE THE MOON A SYMBOLIC AND RITUALISTIC SIGNIFICANCE. FOR THEM IT STOOD FOR SILVER AND WAS USED TO DEPICT THAT METAL IN THEIR SECRET WRITINGS.

ABOVE LEFT To the alchemists, the moon was a symbol of the metal silver. To Freemasons, however, it is the second of the Lesser Lights of the lodge.

ABOVE RIGHT To the Freemasons, the moon is a symbol of regularity, associated with the way phases of the moon are used to measure the passage of time.

In alchemy, stylized drawings of the sun and the moon with human faces were among the most frequently used images. Early Masonic tracing boards utilized practically the same symbols, so it is clear that, in this respect at least, the first Speculative Freemasons owed a debt to their predecessors, even if there are no direct links between the Craft and that forerunner of modern science. Other images which are used in Freemasonry, such as depictions of the Plumb, Square, Level, Rough Ashlar and Perfect Ashlar, similarly made their first documented appearances in alchemical texts.

THE LESSER LIGHTS

References to the sun, moon and Master of the Lodge as the three Lesser Lights of Freemasonry appear to have originated in the so-called Antient Grand Lodge in England after the split with the original Premier Grand Lodge, which took place in the mid-eighteenth century. American Masonry, in particular, was quick to adopt the Antient interpretation.

In the First Degree initiation ceremony, the moon is identified as the biblical ruler of the night. In a more general symbolic context, it is also associated with the lodge's Senior Warden,

who is positioned to the west of the lodge's Master during such rituals. According to some Masonic commentators, just as the moon's light is a reflection of that of the sun, the Senior Warden reflects the light of the lodge's Master. In this context, it is also significant that the Junior Deacon, who acts as the messenger of the Senior Warden within the lodge, wears the Square and Compasses, enclosing the moon as his Masonic jewel.

MOON LODGES

The moon has a practical as well as a symbolic relevance in Freemasonry although, perhaps paradoxically, this has only heightened the confusion that exists among many non-Masons as to its Masonic significance. Back in the early days of the Craft, it was literally a beacon that Masons could use to help them find the way home in the dark after lodge meetings, particularly in rural areas. Hence the practice grew up of holding lodge meetings during the week of the full moon. Such lodges became referred to as moon lodges.

ALCHEMY AND MASONRY

The alchemists were a group of mystics dating from around the twelfth century, and the forerunners of modern chemists. One of their key beliefs was that base metals, such as lead, could be turned into precious ones. But they were also philosophers who used symbols and drawings extensively in their teachings. Much of the graphic symbolism in Masonry, such as the images of the Plumb, Square, Level, Rough Ashlar and Perfect Ashlar, owe their existence to earlier alchemical texts and writings.

From this, it is easy to see how the notion of Masons as moon worshippers could have arisen. Now, however, the number of such lodges is in steep decline as the need for setting the date of meetings according to the phases of the moon rather than on fixed days has disappeared.

ABOVE Observing the phases of the moon. It was the medieval alchemists who gave the moon graphic and ritualistic importance.

BELOW A humanized moon surrounded by stars often features on Masonic Tracing Boards.

THE GLOBES

THERE ARE TWO GLOBES ASSOCIATED WITH THE RITES OF THE CRAFT. MASONS BELIEVE THE ORIGINS OF THESE GLOBES COULD BE TRACED BACK TO THE TWIN COLUMNS THAT STOOD AT THE ENTRANCE TO KING SOLOMON'S TEMPLE, A GLOBE RESTING ON EACH. THE CELESTIAL GLOBE SYMBOLIZED THE SPIRITUAL PART OF HUMAN NATURE WHILE THE TERRESTRIAL GLOBE SYMBOLIZED THE MATERIAL SIDE. THEIR PRESENCE AT MASONIC LODGES TODAY EMPHASIZES THAT THE BELIEF IN FREEMASONRY IS UNIVERSAL.

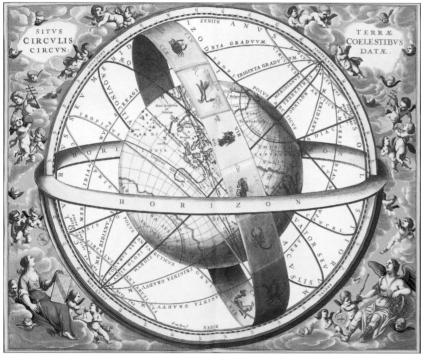

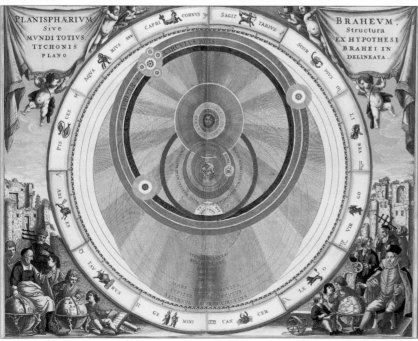

According to the Masonic lecture traditionally delivered on the subject of the Second Tracing Board, there were "two great pillars that were placed in the porchway entrance on the south side…they were formed hollow, the better to serve as archives for Freemasonry, for therein were deposited the Constitutional Rolls…these pillars were adorned with two chapters…with two spheres on which were delineated maps of the celestial and terrestrial globes, pointing out 'Masonry Universal'." It is a nice description but pure mythology.

Unfortunately, there is absolutely no proof that globes surmounted Solomon's columns – or, indeed, that they were hollow – though it is thought possible that they might have been decorated with bronze bowls, the precise purpose of which remains unknown. Indeed, there is not even a mention of the columns in the Old Charges, though Solomon and David, his father, are named as being among the people who "loved Masons well".

Globes were adopted as headpieces to the columns some time during the eighteenth century, but there is no evidence to show that they formed any part of the Masonic catechism or ritual before

ABOVE LEFT Tycho Brahe's system of planetary orbits. The first reference to astronomy in Freemasonry comes in the Cooke Manuscript, one of the Old Charges.

LEFT The situation of the earth in the heavens – another way of stressing the Craft's universality.

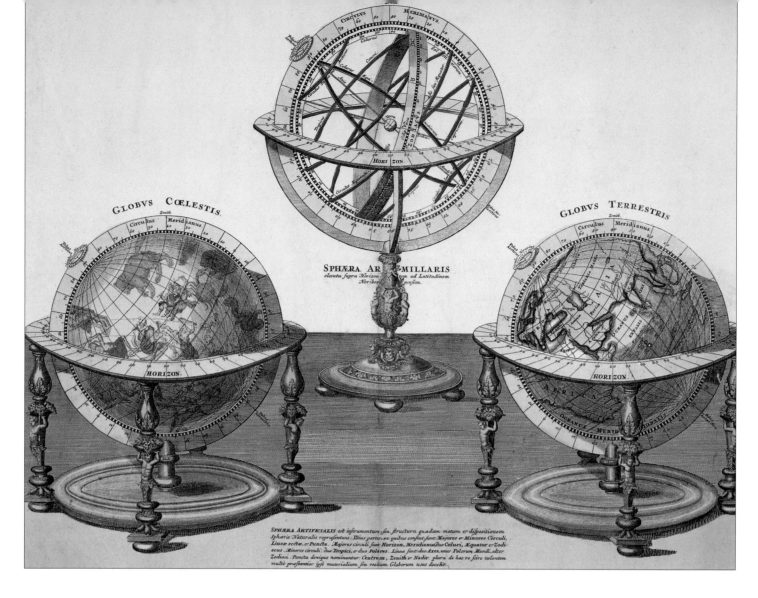

around 1745. It was then, it seems, that spheres or globes first started to appear in Masonic floor drawings and on Tracing Boards. As far as Solomon's columns are concerned, the first records of globes appearing on them date from the 1760s and 1770s.

Whenever it happened, the introduction of the two globes came about slowly and was by no means consistent. Sometimes, the globes stood separately on four-legged or tripod stands to the left and right of the Master of the Lodge's pedestal. It seems that in many lodges, the globes formed a part of lodge equipment in their own right while in others, they found no place at all.

GLOBES AND MAPS

It also seems likely that the tradition of globes featuring celestial and terrestrial maps is late eighteenth century rather than Biblical in origin.

In its 1775 edition, *The Illustrations of Masonry* deals at some length with the nature of the globes, the spiritual and moral lessons to be learned from them, and the importance of astronomy in Freemasonry, but it is not until 1802 that there is any confirmation that maps appear on them and that the latter have any part in Masonic symbolism, allegory or ritual.

ABOVE Globes of the kind found in many Masonic lodges in the early nineteenth century. They were always paired – one celestial and one terrestrial.

PRESTON AND THE GLOBES

It was William Preston in his *The Illustrations of Masonry*, first published in 1775, who first made detailed and specific reference to terrestrial and celestial globes. He defined them as "the noblest instruments for giving us the most distinct idea of any problems or propositions, as well as for enabling us to solve it". He went on to stress the morals to be learned from their study. Symbolically, their meanings included those of wisdom and understanding.

THE MOSAIC PAVEMENT

THE PAVEMENT IS ONE OF THE THREE ORNAMENTS OF A MASONIC LODGE, ALONG WITH THE BLAZING
STAR AND THE INDENTED TESSEL. THE PAVEMENT ITSELF CONSISTS OF AN INLAID PATTERN OF
ALTERNATING SMALL BLACK AND WHITE SQUARES TO SUGGEST THE DUALISTIC ELEMENTS OF DAY AND
NIGHT. VIEWS AS TO THE PAVEMENT'S DEEPER SYMBOLIC SIGNIFICANCE DIFFER — SOME BELIEVE, THAT
IT IS EMBLEMATIC OF HUMAN LIFE, OTHERS THAT IT REPRESENTS THE TWO SIDES OF EVERYTHING, SUCH
AS BLACK AND WHITE, ACTIVE AND PASSIVE, OR EASY AND DIFFICULT.

In Freemasonry the Mosaic Pavement is first and
foremost a representation of the ground floor
of King Solomon's Temple. Attempts have been
made to trace its origins back to the time of the
ancient Egyptians. In the *Mysteries of Freemasonry*,
for instance, the term "mosaic" is said to be
derived from the Egyptian word meaning "saved
or disengaged from the waters", which was used
to describe the nine months of the year during
which the Nile was not in flood. The variegated
appearance of the land during the early part
of this season, with fields of grain intersected
at regular intervals by irrigation canals, was
reproduced in temple architecture by the
tessellated pavement and the same word
was naturally used to describe it.

INTERPRETING THE SYMBOLISM
In Masonic parlance, the Mosaic Pavement is
termed "the beautiful floor" of the lodge, the
border is "the skirtwork", and the Blazing Star
is "the glory in the centre". The Pavement itself is
said to represent the earthly aspects of mankind's
existence and the trials and tribulations of
everyday life. It is called "beautiful" because it is
variegated and chequered in colour and design as
a reminder of the eternal sequence of day and

LEFT A depiction of an early temple, with plenty of
Masonic imagery surrounding the entrance and an
early variation of the Masonic Pavement.

night as well as the varied nature of the objects that decorate and adorn Creation as a whole.

Various interpretations have been put forward to explain the Pavement's undoubted symbolism. Some say that it symbolizes "the chequered life of man" and some that it "represents a life made up of good and evil". Others hold that it shows "the joys and sorrows of life". Perhaps the best explanation is that it is a synthesis of opposites.

THE INDENTED TESSEL

The tessellated border or skirting that surrounds the Mosaic Pavement is called the Indented Tessel. This border, according to Masonic commentaries, symbolizes "those blessings and comforts that surround us and that we hope to obtain by a faithful reliance on Divine Providence, which is hieroglyphically represented by the Blazing Star in the centre".

In what is termed its lesser aspect, the Indented Tessel refers to the planets in their orbits around the sun, but in its more important aspect, it refers to the canopy of stars that surrounds the universe. What the symbolism stresses is the inherent insignificance of humanity unless guided by the strength and wisdom of the Supreme Being.

INTERPRETING THE SQUARES

Explanations of what the Mosaic Pavement symbolizes vary. The standard view is that it is emblematic of human life, chequered with good and evil. Others hold the view that the squares represent day and night.

ABOVE This Tracing Board shows the Mosaic Pavement and the idea of progress towards eventual enlightenment.

ABOVE TOP LEFT This Tracing Board shows the Mosaic Pavement with the two pillars of the Temple in the foreground.

STAIRS AND LADDERS

PLAYING A MAJOR ROLE IN THE RITUALS THAT ACCOMPANY ADMISSION TO THE SECOND DEGREE, THE WINDING STAIRCASE REPRESENTS MAN'S INSTINCTS TO RISE, EXCEL AND EXPLORE THE UNKNOWN. CLIMBING THE STAIRCASE, IT IS SAID, MARKS HIS PROGRESS ALONG THE SPIRITUAL PATH AS HE EXPANDS AND FINDS OUT HOW TO MAKE FULL USE OF HIS INTELLECTUAL FACULTIES. JACOB'S LADDER FEATURES IN THE FIRST DEGREE INITIATION CEREMONY. IT SYMBOLIZES THE LESSONS LEARNED IN LIFE, WHICH, IF PROPERLY EMPLOYED, INCREASE THE SUM OF OUR KNOWLEDGE. THE LADDER DERIVES ITS NAME AND SYMBOLISM FROM JACOB'S VISION OF A LADDER LEADING UPWARDS TO HEAVEN, AS RELATED IN GENESIS.

RIGHT A late eighteenth-century Irish silver jewel. In most of the Ancient Mysteries, the ladder was a symbol of advancement.

BELOW In this Second Degree Tracing Board, the ladder has become a winding stairway leading to the inner sanctum of the Masonic Temple.

OPPOSITE In the Bible, a weary Jacob lays down and dreams of a ladder or stairway reaching to Heaven. In Freemasonry both the rungs and the whole are symbolic.

For a Fellow Craft candidate, the Winding Staircase is a sign that it is time to embark on the search for divine truth. As he ascends the stairs, he makes two pauses. During the first of these, he learns about the "peculiar organization" of the Masonic Order. This is intended to remind the initiate of the union of men in society, the blessings of civilization and the fruits of virtue. When he pauses for the second time, he receives instruction about the human senses and architecture. The

former symbolize intellectual cultivation, while the latter reminds him of the need to cultivate practical knowledge.

According to Masonic teaching, the initiate is embarking on the tortuous climb toward the goal of achievement. No one can see in advance what lies at the top of a winding staircase – the climb must be completed in order to discover it. Hence, there is also the challenge of the unknown to be conquered.

JACOB'S LADDER

Probably introduced into Speculative Freemasonry in the mid-eighteenth century in England (the ladder does not feature in Continental Masonry), Jacob's Ladder may have come from Hermeticism, in which it was a familiar symbol. The steps each have a meaning – the first symbolizes Justice, the second Equality, the third Kindness, the fourth Good Faith, the Fifth Labour, the sixth Patience and the seventh Intelligence. Another interpretation is that they represent Justice, Charity, Innocence, Sweetness, Faith, Firmness and Truth. Taken as a whole, the symbolism seems to point to the connection between faith and heaven, or, as it is declared in Masonic teaching, "Faith in God, Charity to All Men and Hope in Immortality."

JACOB'S DREAM

In his dream of a ladder connecting Earth with Heaven, God promised Jacob his protection and confirmed his pledge to Abraham that the chosen people would possess the whole of the land from the Euphrates River to the south-west. Jacob commemorated the dream by setting up as a monument the stone on which he had rested his head, pouring oil over it to mark the place where he knew that God was present.

In Freemasonry, the ladder always has seven rungs, each representing a particular theological or social virtue. Other ladders also feature in the additional Degrees of the Craft. One, symbolizing the trials and agonies suffered by Jesus Christ, is ascended in the search for the Lost Word. Another mysterious ladder refers to a Mason's moral duties to God, his fellows and humanity as a whole, while a third prescribes the seven liberal arts and sciences all Masons are bound to pursue.

RIGHT Irish Masonic jewels. The ladders shown represent faith in God, charity and the hope of immortality.

BELOW The Degrees of Freemasonry, from an Entered Apprentice at the bottom to the Order of the Temple at the top.

There are two explanations as to why there is an odd number of steps. According to the Roman architect and writer Vitruvius, most ancient temples had odd-numbered steps. The notion was that anyone climbing them would necessarily arrive at the top with the same foot as the one they had started with at the bottom. This was considered to be a good omen. It could also be because, in the Pythagorean system, odd numbers were thought to be more perfect than even ones, so the use of odd-numbered steps symbolized the state of perfection an initiate to the First Degree was expected to attain.

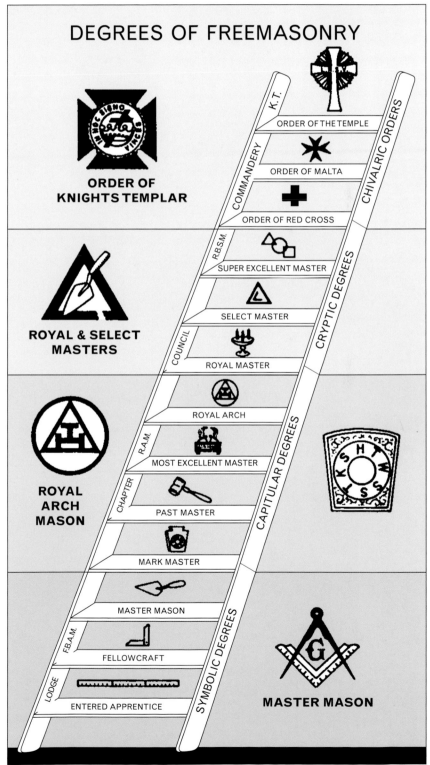

DEGREES OF FREEMASONRY

ORDER OF KNIGHTS TEMPLAR

K.T.

ORDER OF THE TEMPLE

ORDER OF MALTA

ORDER OF RED CROSS

COMMANDERY

CHIVALRIC ORDERS

ROYAL & SELECT MASTERS

R.B.S.M.

SUPER EXCELLENT MASTER

SELECT MASTER

ROYAL MASTER

COUNCIL

CRYPTIC DEGREES

ROYAL ARCH MASON

ROYAL ARCH

R.A.M.

MOST EXCELLENT MASTER

PAST MASTER

CHAPTER

MARK MASTER

CAPITULAR DEGREES

MASTER MASON

F.B.A.M.

FELLOWCRAFT

ENTERED APPRENTICE

LODGE

SYMBOLIC DEGREES

MASTER MASON

THE COFFIN AND SKULL

FOR ANTI-MASONIC POLEMICISTS, THE PRESENCE OF A COFFIN AND A SKULL IN THE SYMBOLIST PANTHEON MORE THAN JUSTIFIES THE CLAIM THAT FREEMASONRY IS BASICALLY UNGODLY AND EVEN SATANIC IN INSPIRATION, HAVING ITS ROOTS IN PAGANISM AND THE OCCULT. WHY, THEY ASK, SHOULD MASONS UTILIZE A SYMBOL WHOSE CLASSIC MEANING, AS IN THE CASE OF THE SKULL AND CROSSBONES, IS DEATH, POISON OR DANGER? WHY WOULD THEY NEED A SYMBOL OF MORTALITY? SUCH VIEWS, HOWEVER, ARE BASED ON A FUNDAMENTAL MISINTERPRETATION OF WHAT FREEMASONRY IS AND WHAT THE MEANING AND PURPOSE OF ITS RITUALS ACTUALLY ARE.

ABOVE The Skull and Crossbones originally made their appearance in French Freemasonry as a symbol of both death and mortality.

RIGHT From *The Perfect Ceremonies of Craft Freemasonry,* 1874, this illustrates the Opening of the Lodge at the beginning of the Third Degree initiation ceremony in which the coffin is prominent.

Freemasonry is not a religion and promotes no doctrine or dogma as anti-Masonic polemicists would have people believe. The "search for light" is a reference to the Masons' continued quest for knowledge rather than salvation. Though the Craft promotes the hope of resurrection, it does not teach such a belief.

The ritual governing admission to the Third Degree – this is where the Coffin and Skull appear – includes references to the "immortality of the soul", but this is merely a poetical allusion. If anything, Freemasonry teaches that death is a "mysterious veil that the eye of human reason cannot penetrate" and supports the hope, not the promise, of resurrection.

PLACE IN RITUAL

Like many Masonic symbols, the Coffin and the Skull seem to have made their first appearance some time in the eighteenth century. Certainly, the Coffin is depicted on Tracing Boards of the time. It symbolizes death (the skull and crossbones found originally in French Freemasonry has the double symbolism of death and mortality). Their function is to act as symbols during the ritual re-enactment of the murder of Hiram Abif in the rites that accompany initiation into the Third Degree. In them, "the Maul is that by which our Grand Master was slain; the Spade that which dug

The lesson of the legend is not resurrection, however. It is the steadfastness and fidelity of Hiram Abif before his death that is significant, not what happened after it. That is the background to the various secret signs, grips and tokens by which a Master Mason is identified.

LEFT A nineteenth-century Masonic seal showing a skull, crossbones, coffin, and acacia plant.

BELOW A Third Degree Tracing Board helps initiates to understand the significance of the admission ritual.

his grave; the Coffin that which received his lifeless remains; and the Sprig of Acacia that which bloomed at the head of his grave".

According to Harold Waldwin Percival in *Masonry and its Symbols in the Light of 'Thinking and Destiny'*, from 1952, the process starts with an introduction by the Master of the Lodge. Then the initiate's gaze "is directed down in the darkness to an open grave. Inside is a human skull resting on a pair of crossed thighbones." This part of the ritual ends when the candidate is told that "Even in this perishable frame, there resides a vital and immovable principle, which inspires a holy confidence that the Lord of Life will enable us to trample the King of Terrors beneath our feet and lift our eyes to that bright morning star whose rising brings peace and tranquillity to the faithful and obedient of the human race."

THIRD DEGREE LECTURE

The Coffin, Setting Maul (hammer) and Spade all feature in the lecture of the Third Degree. The Maul is "an emblem of those casualties and diseases by which our Earthly existence may be terminated", while the Spade and the Coffin "are striking emblems of morality and afford serious reflection for a thinking mind". The lecture closes with an injunction to "welcome the grim tyrant Death and receive him as a kind messenger sent from our Supreme Grand Master".

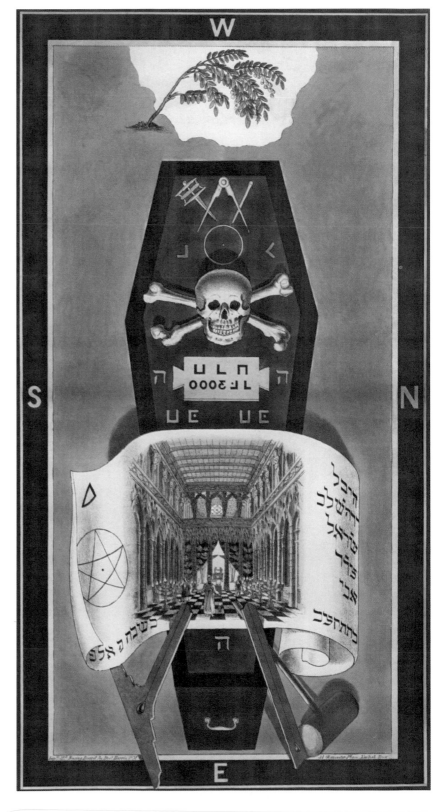

Swords and Daggers

In the eighteenth century, swords were considered a part of everyday dress — at least, for gentlemen — so it is not surprising to find that they feature in the Masonic rituals that were being laid down during that period. Today, however, the wearing of a sword as part of Masonic dress is confined to the Advanced Degrees of orders such as the York Rite. In Blue Lodge or Symbolic Freemasonry its appearance, except as a symbol, is prohibited.

LEFT An elaborately marked Masonic ceremonial sword. Throughout history, swords have been instruments of justice, truth, equality and firmness. They feature symbolically in many Masonic ceremonies.

As a symbol, the Sword has a classic duality to it. In most cultures, any weapon symbolizes power, but this power can be used in different ways. On the one hand, it can kill and destroy, but on the other, it can protect, defend and counter injustice. This is why swords are often symbolically double-edged. They are also closely linked to light. The Crusaders used to call them "fragments of the Cross of Light".

THE TYLER'S SWORD

Traditionally, the Tyler's Sword should have a wavy blade because it is considered to be a symbol of the flaming sword that, according to Genesis, was placed at the east of the Garden of Eden to protect the Tree of Life. It should never be sheathed as in Freemasonry it is the Tyler's duty to keep all "cowens and eavesdroppers" out of the lodge at all times. It is also a perpetual reminder that nothing unworthy should ever be permitted within the sanctuary of the lodge and the fact that, for every Mason, the Tyler and his drawn sword symbolize the need to be perpetually on guard against the approach of unworthy thoughts and deeds and always remembering the Masonic virtues in the face of enemies. It is also the guardian of the *Book of Constitutions*.

THE BOOK OF CONSTITUTIONS

Guarded by the Tyler's Sword, the *Book of Constitutions* reminds Masons that they "should be ever watchful and guarded in our thoughts, words and actions, particularly when before the enemies of Masonry, ever bearing in mind those truly Masonic virtues, silence and circumspection."

FAR LEFT In this Masonic medal design, the sword of truth and justice is resting on the altar, directly under the Blazing Star.

THE DAGGER IN RITUAL

Daggers have a specific part to play in Masonic initiation ritual. When a candidate for the First Degree arrives at the lodge, he finds the door guarded by a swordsman, who knocks at the door with the hilt of his drawn sword to ask permission for the candidate to enter. The latter is then hoodwinked – blindfolded – and dressed in a loose-fitting pair of trousers and a white tunic. He wears one slipper, his left leg is bared to the knee, and the left side of the tunic pushed back to expose his left breast. Any metal objects he may be carrying are taken away from him. A hangman's noose is then placed around the candidate's neck and he is led, still blindfold, into the Lodge Room. There, the point of a dagger is pressed to his chest while he undergoes ritual questioning. Once this is over, the dagger point is removed, the candidate kneels, and a prayer is chanted. The initiation ceremony then proceeds through its various other stages, including the customary three perambulations around the lodge, to its conclusion.

BELOW A nineteenth-century First Degree initiation ceremony, in which a dagger is pressed against the candidate's breast while he is being questioned.

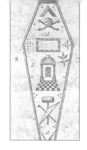

GEOMETRIC SHAPES

GIVEN FREEMASONRY'S OBSESSION WITH THE WORK OF PYTHAGORAS AND EUCLID AND WITH GEOMETRY IN GENERAL, IT IS HARDLY SURPRISING THAT GEOMETRIC SHAPES FEATURE PROMINENTLY IN MASONIC SYMBOLISM. MASONS HAVE ALWAYS BELIEVED THAT THE CRAFT AND GEOMETRY ARE INTERTWINED AND THAT A PROPER UNDERSTANDING OF THE LATTER PROVIDES THE MEANS TO AN UNDERSTANDING OF THE FORMER. THIS BELIEF GOES BACK AT LEAST TO THE DAYS OF THE OLD CHARGES. A DOCUMENT DATED 1583 STATES THAT GEOMETRY "TEACHETH A NAB THE METT AND MEASURE OF EARTH AND ALL OTHER THINGS".

Much later, the Masonic authority Thomas Smith Webb was to write: "Geometry, the first and noblest of the sciences, is the basis on which the superstructure of Freemasonry is erected. By Geometry, we may curiously trace Nature through her various windings to her most concealed recesses. By it, we discover the power, the wisdom and the goodness of the Grand Artificer of the Universe and view with delight the proportions that connect this vast machine."

BELOW This eighteenth-century image includes a reference to Pythagoras' theorem at its centre.

THE RECTANGLE

One of the most significant elements of the Tracing Board is the enclosing rectangle, whose proportions follow the precepts of the "golden section" to the letter, and is one of the key features of geometry as originated by the Pythagorean school. At its simplest, the golden section, or ratio, is a simple rectangle whose proportions represent a mathematical sequence.

THE TRIANGLE

In Masonry a triangle can be formed out of the three Hebrew characters "He" or the three 5s. The symbol has several possible interpretations, the first of which is mystical. From ancient times, the equilateral triangle was an emblem of God and a symbol of perfection, which can be attained only by passing through the Valley of the Shadow of Death. This is why the apex of the triangle points downwards. Similarly, the sum of the three "Hes" forming the triangle is 15, considered a sacred number that symbolizes the name of God.

The temporal interpretation relates to the individual in his natural environment and his civic obligations and duties. The first character in the triangle represents the five elements – earth, air, water, fire and the ether. The second represents the five senses and the third concerns the moral responsibility whereby every Mason has to help fellow Masons in times of trouble and to support them in their endeavours. There are also three possible collective interpretations that appear in Freemasonry. In the first, the three "Hes" are the initial letters of the three Hirams who helped King Solomon in the planning of, supply of raw materials for and building of his temple. In the second, the characters refer to the 15 trusted craftsmen who were sent by the king to search for Hiram Abif in three groups of five after disappearing. Finally, Speculative Masons believe the characters represent the five perfect points of entrance in the Three Degrees – Token, Preparation, Obligation, Sign and Word.

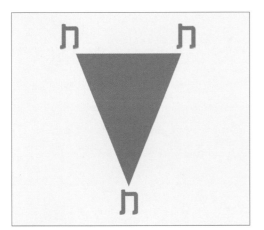

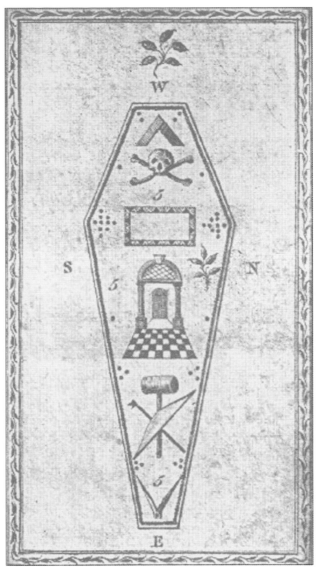

FAR LEFT The three "Hes" form an inverted triangle. The sum of the three is 15, symbolizing the name of God. In the temporal interpretation the first character is in the apex, and the second and third are represented in a clockwise direction.

LEFT The Third or Master Mason's Degree Tracing Board includes an enclosed rectangle, whose ratios conform to the "golden section".

ABOVE The Jewel of a Past Master shows the significance of Pythagoras' theorem and of the propositions of Euclid in Freemasonry.

GEOMETRIC MASON'S MARKS

It has been suggested that when a great building was planned a complex "mother-diagram" was drawn and Mason's Marks allotted to the Masons employed – as represented by geometric shapes. A Viennese architect Franz Rziha claimed to have found evidence of Mason's Marks in German and Austrian towns and cities and published his findings at the end of the nineteenth century.

SYMBOLIC CITIES

SIGNS AND SYMBOLS

ORIGINALLY, THE FREEMASONS WERE AN ORGANIZATION OF MASTER BUILDERS, BOUND TOGETHER BY THEIR CLOSELY GUARDED KNOWLEDGE OF "THE EARTHLY AND DIVINE SCIENCES" OF ARCHITECTURE. THE UNDERSTANDING OF HOW AN EARTHLY STRUCTURE WAS BUILT WOULD PROVIDE THE WISDOM FOR BUILDING A SPIRITUAL TEMPLE WITHIN THE SOUL. UNSURPRISINGLY, THE MASONIC ACHIEVEMENT IN PLANNING AND BUILDING HAS BEEN SUBSTANTIAL. WHILE THERE IS LITTLE EVIDENCE OF MASONIC MASTER PLANS FOR BUILDING CITIES, THERE ARE SOME WHO CLAIM THAT SYMBOLIC SHAPES MADE BY THE POSITIONING OF STREETS INDICATE THAT MASONIC PLANNING HAS BEEN AT WORK.

BELOW Planning the city and tower of Babel. This was most likely to be a Masonic enterprise, though there is no historical evidence to support this belief.

If anti-Masonic propaganda is to be believed, the greatest coup of Freemasonry was to dictate the planning and building of Washington DC as the capital of the newly independent United States. Unfortunately, this is not the case. It is true that many of the city's architects in the nineteenth and early twentieth centuries were Masons. Yet although George Washington, who commissioned Pierre Charles L'Enfant to draw up the original plan for the city in 1791 and later approved the street plan suggested by Andrew Ellicott and Benjamin Bannaker, was a Mason, none of these architects was a member of the Craft.

The notion that some grand Masonic conspiracy lay behind the city's planning seems to stem from Michael Baigent and Richard Leigh's 1989 book *The Temple and the Lodge*. In this title they claim that Washington and Thomas Jefferson interfered with L'Enfant's work to impose a pair of octagonal shapes around the White House and the Capitol. There is no documentary evidence to support the claim. What seems more likely is that the founding fathers of the city were more inspired by André Le Nôtre's designs for the palace of Versailles and Sir

THE TOWER OF BABEL

According to the Book of Genesis, it was the descendants of Noah who got the idea of building a vast tower or ziggurat, "the top of which may reach to Heaven". Their purpose was "to make our name famous", but God confounded their tongues and the tower was abandoned.

RIGHT Masonic architects. The notion that Masons built the cities of the ancient world, as suggested here, was a speculative idea that was common in eighteenth-century Freemasonry.

BELOW RIGHT The streets of the city of Sandusky, Ohio, are laid out according to an early nineteenth-century Masonic master plan, so that they form a picture of the Square and Compasses.

Christopher Wren's unexecuted plans for London than they were by Freemasonry. L'Enfant's plans featured two focal points – the Capitol and the White House – while the expansive axial boulevards and the monumental architecture employed were intended as a monument to the "Virtuous Citizen in the New Republic".

The decisive feature in the positioning of major buildings was topography. The intersections of Massachusetts Avenue, Rhode Island Avenue, Connecticut Avenue, Vermont Avenue and K Street NW do indeed form a five-pointed star. However, it is far more likely this was coincidence rather than a Masonic conspiracy.

A MASONIC CITY

The story is different in Sandusky, Ohio, which is the only city in the world as far as is known to have been laid out according to a Masonic master plan. Hector Kilbourne, the first Master of Science Lodge No. 50, was the surveyor who drew up the city plan in 1818. He took great care to position the streets so as to form a picture of the Square and Compasses. Indeed, his plan for the city as a whole has been likened to a representation of an open Bible, with the Square and Compasses in the positions they would be in at the opening of a meeting of a Masonic Lodge. Some of the street names honour statesmen and other prominent members of the country in the history of the United States.

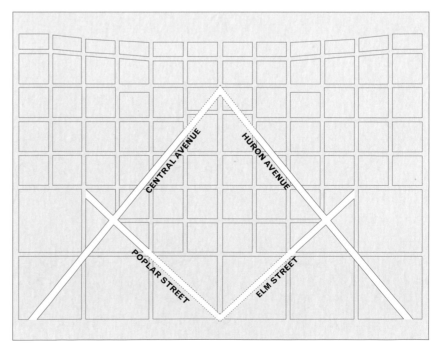

BOOK, BEES AND BEEHIVE

THE OPEN BOOK IS A RELATIVELY RECENT INTRODUCTION TO FREEMASONRY; WHILE THE BEES AND BEEHIVE HAVE MUCH OLDER ORIGINS, THE BOOK IS PART OF THE SYMBOLISM ATTACHED TO THE STORY OF THE BROKEN COLUMN, WHICH MOST MASONIC AUTHORITIES AGREE MADE ITS FIRST APPEARANCE IN THE *TRUE MASONIC CHART* COMPILED BY AMERICAN MASON JEREMY CROSS IN 1819.

THE BROKEN COLUMN AND OPEN BOOK
The notion of the Broken Column came about after Jeremy Cross found or sensed a deficiency in the Third Degree rituals that he was determined to correct. The idea of what this correction could be came to him after a friend commented that a monument was generally built to commemorate great men after their death. Cross accepted the suggestion, taking the idea for his symbolic image from the monument that had been erected to the American naval hero Commodore Lawrence in Trinity Churchyard, New York, following his death in battle with the British in 1813. Cross decided that an Open Book, supposedly recounting Hiram Abif's life, should be placed upon the pillar with a beautiful virgin – an emblem of innocence – depicted weeping over it as she reads. The Broken Column is also said to represent the untimely death of Hiram Abif and Solomon's unfinished temple.

ABOVE The Open Book. The book is said to lie open on the Broken Column so that Hiram Abif's virtues lie on perpetual record.

RIGHT A statue of the Broken Column with Father Time comforting the Weeping Virgin. She is holding an acacia leaf symbolizing hope.

Invention and knowledge did not go hand in hand, however. Not only were there no books in existence — at least, as we understand them — at the time when King Solomon's Temple was built, there is also no scriptural account of Hiram having a wife, daughter or any female relative other than his mother — he is described in the Bible as "a widow's son". Nevertheless, Masons believe that the symbol has a place in their traditions, even if it has romance, rather than fact, behind it.

BEES AND THE BEEHIVE

Having made their appearance in Egyptian, Roman and Christian symbolism, the Bee and the Beehive had more ancient pedigrees before they became part of Freemasonry. In the eighteenth century Freemasonry adopted the beehive as a symbol of industry; bees and beehives also symbolize wisdom, obedience and regeneration. Since then the symbols frequently appear in Masonic illustration. According to Albert G. Mackey's *Encyclopaedia of Freemasonry*, the reasons Masons should "go to the bee and learn how diligent she is and what a noble work she produces" is because "though weak in strength, yet since she values wisdom she prevails".

In the *True Masonic Chart*, as well as being "an emblem of industry", the beehive "teaches us that, as we came into the world rational and intelligent beings, so we should ever be industrious ones, never sitting down contented while our fellow creatures around us are in want, when it is in our power to relieve them without inconvenience to ourselves". The parallel here is the instructions given to a Master Mason as part of the initiation rituals of the Third Degree. These state that a Master Mason "works that he may receive wages, the better to support himself and his family, and contribute to the relief of a worthy, distressed brother, his widow and orphans".

BEEHIVES AND SYMBOLISM
The Beehive has had a place in Egyptian, Roman and Christian symbolism. As a Masonic symbol it teaches us that "Industry is a virtue that should be practised by all created beings, from the highest seraph in the Heavens to the lowest reptile in the dust."

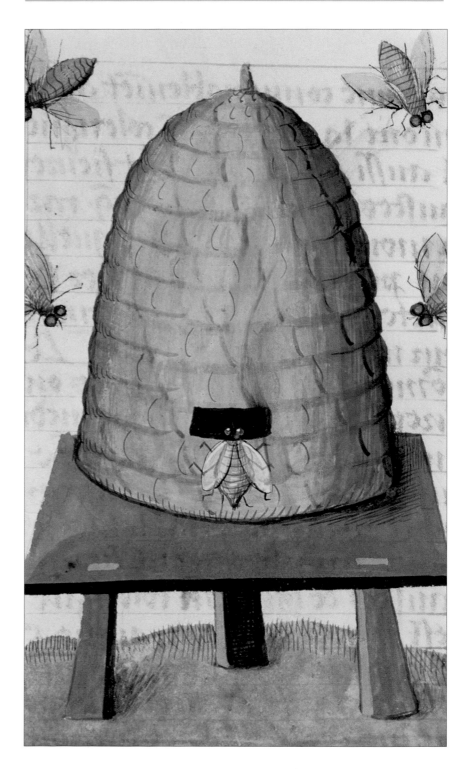

ABOVE Bees returning to the hive. In Freemasonry, the bee is a symbol of industry, obedience and rebirth. It is an appropriate emblem for systematized industry, a virtue taught in the instructions.

LIFE, TIME AND JUSTICE

BOTH THE HOUR GLASS AND THE SCYTHE ARE EMBLEMS THAT FEATURE IN THE RITUALS OF THIRD DEGREE FREEMASONRY, PRIMARILY IN THE UNITED STATES. THE FORMER IS A SYMBOL OF HUMAN LIFE, WHILE THE LATTER IS AN EMBLEM OF TIME, WHICH "CUTS THE BRITTLE THREAD OF LIFE AND LAUNCHES US INTO ETERNITY". TOGETHER, THEY BECOME SYMBOLS OF THE IMPORTANCE OF SPENDING TIME PROFITABLY IN THE SERVICE OF GOD. THE SCALES SYMBOLIZE JUSTICE. THEY ARE INTRODUCED INTO FREEMASONRY IN THE FIRST DEGREE RITUALS, WHERE, ALONG WITH TEMPERANCE, FORTITUDE AND PRUDENCE, THEY FORM THE FOUR CARDINAL VIRTUES.

BELOW The Hour Glass symbolizes human life and its brevity, while the Scythe is an emblem of time and immortality. The message is clear – to make the best use of the time at our disposal.

THE HOUR GLASS

This was probably chosen as the symbol for human life because by its very nature, the Hour Glass is an indication of brevity. Time, so Masonic logic tells us, is the only resource men share in equal abundance. This can be used for fruitful and profitable purposes or it can be squandered. The grains of sand in the Hour Glass pass slowly but surely through it and, before we know it, time is complete. The lesson is that time must be used wisely as time wasted is time lost.

THE SCYTHE

This is a reminder of the certainty of death. While no one can predict when this will be, we must be prepared for an inevitable demise through service to God and to our fellow men. The Scythe is also a symbol of the immortality of the human soul. The unspoken assurance is that, if time is used wisely to acquire knowledge and understanding, which, in turn, is used to serve God and benefit society, then the reward will be great and eternal.

THE SCALES

Justice is one of the Cardinal Virtues. All Freemasons are charged with the necessity of preserving an upright position in all their dealings. This means never failing to act justly in the eyes of their Masonic brethren and those of the world. This is the only cornerstone – another powerful Masonic symbol – on which "a superstructure alike honourable to themselves and to the Fraternity" would be built. This is illustrated in the First Degree rituals, when the candidate for admission is instructed to keep his feet firmly planted on the ground and his body upright.

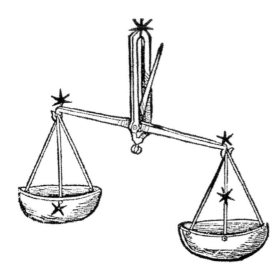

LEFT A symbol of justice, the scales feature in the rituals governing admission to the First Degree together with the other Cardinal Virtues.

BELOW The crucial stage in a First Degree initiation ceremony when the candidate's blindfold is removed as he stands firmly on the ground.

THE OTHER CARDINAL VIRTUES

The three other virtues are just as clearly defined. Temperance means never revealing the secrets with which an initiate is entrusted through overindulgence – or, as the ritual somewhat quaintly puts it, "in the unguarded hours of dissipation". Fortitude is a reminder that any ills that may befall a person in life must be borne "with becoming resignation". It also teaches a candidate for initiation to let "no dangers or pains dissolve the inviolable fidelity he owed to the trusts reposed in him". The fourth virtue in Freemasonry, Prudence, is considered to be "the true guide to human understanding". In American ritual – the English one differs slightly – it consists of "judging and determining with propriety what is to be said or done on all our occasions, what dangers we should endeavor to avoid, and how to act in all our difficulties".

ORIGINS OF THE VIRTUES

Before at least 1750, there is no reference to the Cardinal Virtues in any Masonic manuscript or ritual. What seems the most likely is that the idea was taken from the Christian church, which itself had derived the notion from the teachings of the Greek philosopher Plato. Freemasonry also borrowed the three Theological Virtues – Faith, Hope and Charity – from Christianity. All of these Virtues feature on the rungs of the Masonic version of Jacob's Ladder.

WHEAT AND PLANTS

IN FREEMASONRY, WHEAT, WINE AND OLIVE OIL ARE SYMBOLS OF NOURISHMENT, REFRESHMENT AND JOY. THEY TEACH MASONS AN IMPORTANT LESSON — ALWAYS TO BE READY TO "NOURISH THE NEEDY, REFRESH THE DESTITUTE AND POUR THE OIL OF JOY INTO THE HEARTS OF THE AFFLICTED". KING SOLOMON GAVE CORN, WINE AND OIL TO THE BUILDERS OF HIS TEMPLE AS A REWARD FOR THEIR LABOURS, WHICH IS WHY, IN THE SECOND DEGREE INITIATION RITUALS, NEWLY ADMITTED FELLOW CRAFT MASONS ARE GIVEN THE SAME "WAGES". PLANTS ARE ALSO IMPORTANT ELEMENTS OF MASONIC SYMBOLISM, NOTABLY THE ACACIA.

THE SYMBOLISM OF WHEAT

The use of wheat (corn) as a religious symbol dates back at least to the time of the ancient Greeks, when it was used as the emblem of the goddess Demeter. In the festivals held in her honour, priests and worshippers alike were crowned with ears of wheat. This symbolized the fertility of the earth, which gave bread to mankind. Thus wheat was the personification of the notions of abundance and fertility. Similarly, wine was the symbol of the Greek god Dionysus, while olive oil was a gift to the Greeks from Athena, the goddess of knowledge. It is the symbol of spiritual enlightenment and peace.

In Biblical symbolism the three products possess a similar meaning and significance, while in Christian liturgy, the corn and the wine are echoed by the elements of the Communion service — the bread and wine represent the body and blood of Christ. The oil is a symbol of baptism. In Freemasonry the grain is the reward given in recognition of the efforts the recipient has made in the building of himself and the temple, the wine is a recognition of his discovery of hidden knowledge and the oil a remembrance of the spiritual enlightenment he has achieved.

A SACRED PLANT

Like the wheat, wine and olive oil, the acacia's role as a significant religious symbol dates back to very ancient times indeed.

In the Bible it is referred to as *shittim* and was revered as the sacred wood from which the Ark of the Covenant was made. In Freemasonry it represents the immortality of the soul — this is how it features in the ritual of the Third Degree in the retelling of the murder of Hiram Abif and at Masonic funerals (though in the latter case, the

BELOW Masonic medals from lodges in Hamburg (right) and Geneva (left) both depict significant symbolic plants.

BELOW RIGHT Wheat has long been associated with Freemasonry. In conjunction with wine and oil they play an important part in the dedication, consecration and constitution of a new lodge.

PLANTS, BIRDS AND ANIMALS

Masonic lodges across the world have names associated with plants, birds and animals – the Oak, Walnut Tree, Arboretum, Beehive, Lion and Swan are just a few examples. This dove and olive branch is the emblem of one of the lodge officers – the Grand Deacon in England – the bird symbolizing a messenger and the olive branch purity, peace and innocence. The symbolism derives from the story of Noah and the Great Flood as related in the Book of Genesis where a dove was released from the Ark by Noah and returned with an olive branch.

BELOW The collar worn by the Grand Officers at the Grand Lodge of England showing wheat emblems.

BOTTOM Carpenters at work making the Ark of the Covenant. They used *shittim*, the Hebrew word for acacia, which itself is a highly significant Masonic symbol.

cedar or cypress is often substituted for it). Acacia also symbolizes innocence and initiation. In the former case, the symbolism does not derive from any real analogy but depends on the Greek meaning of the word, which is "innocence" or "freedom from sin". As far as initiation is concerned, the acacia is the Masonic equivalent of the lettuce, lotus, heather, ivy, and mistletoe, all of which were sacred symbols in the Ancient Mysteries of long ago. Lettuce, for instance, was the sacred plant of the mysteries of Adonis, the lotus featured in India's Brahmanical rites, and the Druids and the ancient Egyptians revered myrtle, mistletoe and heather.

THE JEWELS

THE PRACTICE OF WEARING JEWELS STARTED ONLY WHEN THE PREMIER GRAND LODGE RESOLVED THAT ALL MASTERS AND WARDENS OF LODGES HAD TO WEAR JEWELS, OR BADGES OF OFFICE, SUSPENDED BY RIBBONS FROM THEIR NECKS. ACCORDING TO HISTORIANS, MASONIC OFFICERS DID NOT WEAR JEWELS IN THE EARLY DAYS OF SPECULATIVE FREEMASONRY. THE MASTER'S JEWEL IS THE SQUARE, THE SENIOR WARDEN'S THE LEVEL AND THE JUNIOR WARDEN'S THE PLUMB. THE JEWEL OF THE TREASURER IS THE KEY OR CROSSED KEYS – A SYMBOL OF POWER AND AUTHORITY, JUST AS IT WAS AMONG THE ANCIENTS LONG BEFORE THE SYMBOL WAS APPROPRIATED BY THE MASONS.

BELOW In English Freemasonry, the Key (or Crossed Keys) is the emblem or Jewel of Office worn by the Treasurer of the Lodge.

BELOW RIGHT The Secretary of the Lodge's Jewel of Office features two crossed quill pens, which is a particularly appropriate symbol.

FAR RIGHT The Steward is in charge of food, drink and entertainment. His Jewel of Office is a cornucopia.

Today, all lodge officials have their own particular jewel, which is usually made of silver or silver plate. The Secretary, for instance, wears the Crossed Quills, while the Senior and Junior Deacons wear the Square and Compasses with the sun and crescent moon in the centre respectively. The Steward's jewel is a Cornucopia, the Chaplain's the Open Bible, the Tyler's the Sword, the Marshall's Crossed Batons or a Baton, and the Sentinel's the Crossed Swords. Keys appear in the rites of both the Royal Arch Degree and in the Secret Master or Fourth Degree of the Scottish Rite. In these rites the key is a symbol of

secrecy. This serves as a reminder that the secrets of Freemasonry are to be kept locked up or concealed in the heart.

JEWELS OF THE LODGE
Somewhat confusingly, at least to non-Masons, Masonic ritual utilizes the notion of jewels in a different context when it refers to the Jewels of the Lodge. The two, however, are connected.

The Jewels of the Lodge fall into two categories – the Immovable Jewels and the Movable Jewels. In English and Scottish lodges the former consist of the Trestle-board, the Rough Ashlar and

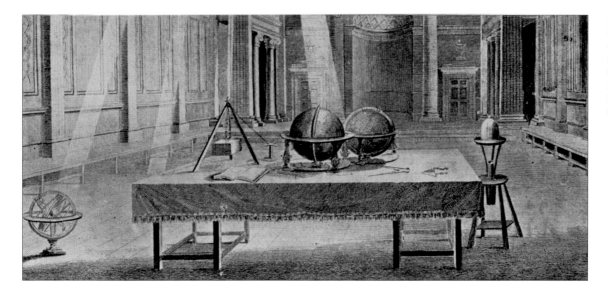

LEFT In most Masonic Lodges, the Perfect Ashlar – one of the Jewels of the Lodge – is suspended from a tripod so that it can be easily seen during meetings and rituals.

the Perfect Ashlar. In North American Masonry the terminology is reversed and the movable jewels are the Ashlars and the Trestle-board. In most lodges, for instance, the Perfect Ashlar is suspended from a tripod positioned to ensure that everybody in the lodge can see it. Once the lodge has been opened, a winch raises the stone manually. This raising is a symbol of the dignity of labour. It is also a reminder of the necessity of working in order to improve the mind.

The Square, Level and Plumb Line are the Movable Jewels in the English and Scottish lodges, and the Immovable Jewels in North America. The Square symbolizes Morality and Justice and so features as the Master of the Lodge's jewel, since it is his duty to ensure that all the members of the lodge conduct themselves morally and justly. The Level as the symbol of Equality is synonymous with the obligations of the Senior Warden, whose job it is to see that all lodge members are treated fairly and in turn, treat each other fairly. Similarly, in standing for Uprightness and Integrity, the Plumb Line is the appropriate jewel for the Junior Warden as he must ensure that his fellow Masons conduct themselves according to these two precepts.

BELOW FAR LEFT The Chaplain's Jewel of Office is a composite image of the Blazing Star, a Triangle and the Holy Bible.

BELOW LEFT The Crossed Swords is the Jewel of Office of the Sentinel, who keeps intruders out while the lodge is meeting.

BELOW The Tyler's Sword traditionally has a curved, twisted blade, though not on this particular Jewel of Office.

THE PENTAGRAM

THE MASONIC SIGNIFICANCE OF THE PENTAGRAM IS CONTROVERSIAL. WHILE IT FREQUENTLY APPEARS ON MASONIC REGALIA AND DECORATIVE ILLUSTRATION, IT IS NOT MENTIONED IN ANY RITUAL, LECTURE OR LESSON. ITS VALUE IS PURELY ORNAMENTAL AND ANY SYMBOLISM ATTACHED TO IT IS AN EXPRESSION OF PERSONAL OPINION. WHEN MASONIC WRITERS TELL US THAT "THE MEDIEVAL FREEMASON CONSIDERED THE PENTAGRAM A SYMBOL OF DEEP WISDOM", THIS IS SPECULATION, NOT TRUTH. SIMILARLY, THE FACT THAT AMONG PYTHAGOREANS THE PENTAGRAM WAS A SYMBOL OF HEALTH AND KNOWLEDGE HAS NO APPLICATION TO FREEMASONRY.

RIGHT A medal to commemorate the centenary of the Grand Master's Lodge features a Pentagram on King Solomon's Temple in the background.

ABOVE An alternative version of the Royal Arch Jewel of Office uses the six-pointed star as its central symbol.

What we do know about the Pentagram is that it was probably first used in the days before recorded history as an emblem for an early Mesopotamian city, and subsequently became a symbol for health and the heavens, an early Christian symbol of the transfigured Christ, and then a medieval talisman to guard against evil. In Hermeticism it became an allegorical symbol of man's relationship with the cosmos. In the Christian context it has been seen as the Alpha and Omega, a symbol of Christ, and as a token of the five wounds the Saviour received upon the Cross.

It is particularly important that this be established, since over the years anti-Masonic polemicists have seized on the supposed significance of the Pentagram as a Masonic symbol to postulate a direct link between the Craft, occult practice, paganism and even Satanism. The Pentagram's transformation from a symbol of good guarding against evil into a symbol representing the latter has been ascribed to many causes. Chief among them, perhaps, was its adoption by herbalists and the like, whose practice of primitive medicine was identified by the ignorant as witchcraft.

FREEMASONRY AND THE PENTAGRAM

Despite numerous attempts to prove the existence of a link, there is absolutely no connection between the Blazing Star of Masonic ritual and the Pentagram. Early Tracing Boards, for instance, depict the star with 16 or 15 points, not the five that would make it a true Pentagram – though there is one notable five-pointed Pentalpha present. Nor have efforts to draw on Masonic veneration for Pythagoras to establish a link between Masonic initiation rites and the Pentagram as a Pythagorean symbol of initiation succeeded. These attempts have also failed to establish any direct or even anecdotal evidence to prove the existence of any such link.

While there are many examples of the Pentagram and five-pointed star being used as stonemasons' marks during the period when the great cathedrals were being built in Europe, there is no proof that they played any part in the genesis of the Craft in the days of Operative

ABOVE The Square and Compasses with a five-pointed star in the centre. This could be derived from the Star of Hermes, which provided light for travellers along the path to eventual enlightenment.

RIGHT This design from seventeenth-century France is a possible prefiguration of the Royal Arch Jewel.

BELOW RIGHT The Great Magic Circle of Agrippa is based on a six-pointed star, which also appears on Masonic badges.

Masonry. If they did, the fact would surely be at least mentioned in the Old Charges. Additionally, although the Pentagram and the five-pointed star can be interpreted as a representation of the Golden Ratio – which is of substantial importance to Masons – whether the early Freemasons thought of this interpretation is again a matter of controversy.

A SYMBOL OF WISDOM

According to Albert G. Mackey, medieval Freemasons considered the Pentagram to be a symbol of deep wisdom. Its first English mention comes in the legend of Sir Gawain and the Green Knight, where Gawain is described as carrying a shield with "shining gules, with the Pentangle in pure gold depicted thereon". This represented the five wounds of Christ and the five virtues of generosity, fellowship, purity, courtesy and mercy.

THE APRON

ONE OF THE MOST VISIBLE SIGNS OF MASONIC MEMBERSHIP IS THE LAMBSKIN OR WHITE LEATHER APRON – "MORE ANCIENT THAN THE GOLDEN FLEECE OR ROMAN EAGLE, MORE HONOURABLE THAN THE STAR AND GARTER OR ANY OTHER ORDER THAT COULD BE CONFERRED AT THIS OR ANY FUTURE PERIOD" – AS THE WORDS OF THE PRESENTATION RITUAL HAVE IT. IT IS THE PERPETUAL SYMBOL OF MASONIC AFFILIATION. WHATEVER A MASON DOES AND WHEREVER HE GOES, THE APRON SERVES TO REMIND HIM OF HIS MASONIC DUTIES AND OBLIGATIONS. IT IS ALSO A SYMBOLIC REMINDER TO HIM TO DO HIS DUTY TO GOD, HIS COUNTRY, HIS NEIGHBOURS AND HIS FAMILY.

BELOW This nineteenth-century Apron contains a wealth of symbolism, including the Temple of Solomon, the Pyramid, the Cedars of Lebanon, the Pillars of Enoch, the Mosaic Pavement, and various Working Tools.

The origins of the Masonic Apron and its early development and character are obscure. Some trace its roots back to the garb worn by the priests of ancient Egypt, but it is more generally held that the leather apron of the Operative Mason found its way into Speculative Freemasonry together with the Working Tools and other symbols of the Craft. As Masonic rituals developed, so the Apron progressed to the place of prominence it holds in Freemasonry today.

SYMBOLS AND DECORATION

According to W. Kirk MacNulty in *Freemasonry – A Journey through Ritual and Symbol* (1991), "the Masonic Apron was an untrimmed white lambskin tied around the waist. This lambskin had been proclaimed by Masonry to be a badge of innocence and purity."

This proclamation was made some time in the eighteenth century, probably around the same time as the practice of decorating Masonic Aprons with symbolic designs began. In Freemasonry symbols are important elements. The most popular symbols included the All-Seeing Eye, the Columns, and the Square and Compasses. The Apron, which was at first a full-length garment, also became physically smaller. Edgings and other forms of ornamentation began to make their appearance, initially in order to make a clear distinction between the plain Apron of an Entered Apprentice and those of a Fellow Craft and a Master Mason.

THE APRON AS A BADGE

As a badge, the Apron means "membership of the Fraternity" and must always be worn in the lodge. It is the "bond of friendship" and so a symbol of

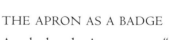

the brotherly virtues. It is the "badge of innocence". It "testifies to or witnesses the honourable age of the Craft". In the Third Degree it is a badge of authority, which gives a Master Mason the right to instruct his juniors.

Some Masons have taken the attempt to discover the significance of all the elements of the Apron to extremes. They go as far as to argue that the form of the Apron and the position of its flap are symbolic. There is little or no justification for such speculation and the same goes for attempts to turn the hook (the circle) and the clasp (the serpent) into significant symbols. The origins of the tassels and their seven chains are also shrouded in mystery. Other decorations are possibly emblematic, but what they mean is impossible to say.

ABOVE President George Washington was a dedicated Mason for much of his life.

LEFT A Grand Master's Apron of white lambskin, the symbol of purity, with gold. The sun is in the centre with seven ears of wheat in each corner.

FAR LEFT This Apron dates from 1772 and features an embroidered triangle. The Apron is an emblem of innocence as well as being the badge of a Freemason.

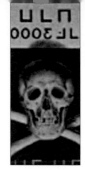

TRACING BOARDS

INTRODUCED INTO FREEMASONRY IN THE LATE EIGHTEENTH CENTURY AS TRAINING DEVICES, TRACING BOARDS WERE — AND STILL ARE — INTENDED TO HELP CANDIDATES TO MASTER THE INTRICATE SYMBOLISM THAT FEATURES IN THE INITIATION RITUALS FOR EACH OF THE THREE DEGREES. THEIR ORIGINS CAN BE TRACED BACK TO THE DAYS WHEN THE PRACTICE WAS FOR THE MASTER OF THE LODGE TO SKETCH DESIGNS ON THE LODGE FLOOR IN CHALK TO ILLUSTRATE THE POINTS HE WAS MAKING IN HIS LECTURES TO THE BRETHREN. THEN CAME FLOOR CLOTHS AND FINALLY, WHEN LODGES STARTED TO ACQUIRE PERMANENT PREMISES, TRACING BOARDS THEMSELVES.

There are individual Tracing Boards for each of the Degrees. Each board is painted with elaborate emblematic diagrams, featuring the key symbols of the respective Degree, the significance of which it is the Master of the Lodge's task to explain. According to W. Kirk MacNulty in *Freemasonry — A Journey through Ritual and Symbol*, the First Degree Board "sets out the general Western metaphysical scheme" and shows the place of the individual within it. The Second Degree Board is a symbolic representation of the individual in more detail,

BELOW Cypher inscriptions on Harris-type Third Degree Boards with their key. They are used to train Masons in the decoding of the secret parts of Masonic ritual.

while the Third Degree Board "alludes to a process…by which the individual can realize a richer interior potential".

THREE BOARDS, THREE DEGREES
In First Degree ritual, indented borders of black and white triangles surround the Board. The main depiction is of a lodge's interior, the central feature being a Mosaic Pavement of black and white tiles. These, like the other elements shown on the Board, represent duality — light and dark, good and evil, and ease and difficulty. The lodge has no walls and is open to the heavens. This is a symbol of the universal nature of the Craft.

Three pillars — one Corinthian, representing Beauty; one Ionic, for Wisdom; and one Doric, for Strength — stand on the Pavement, together with

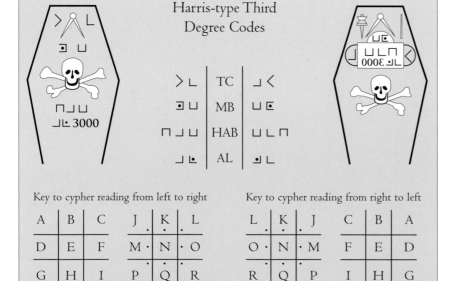

Harris-type Third Degree Codes

Key to cypher reading from left to right

A	B	C		J	K	L
D	E	F		M	N	O
G	H	I		P	Q	R

S		W	
T U		X Y	
V		Z	

Key to cypher reading from right to left

L	K	J		C	B	A
O	N	M		F	E	D
R	Q	P		I	H	G

W		S	
Y X		U T	
Z		V	

INTERPRETING THE CYPHERS

These cyphers, written on the Third Degree Boards, are interpreted using the keys in the illustration. The first line TC is made up of the initials of the password, followed by the letters HAB, the contraction of the name of the main figure in the allegory which makes up the Third Degree. Underneath is the year of the great tragedy, A.L. 3000. AL are the initials of the Latin words, *Anne Lucis*, or Year of Light. In this instance, the light is the Light of Creation.

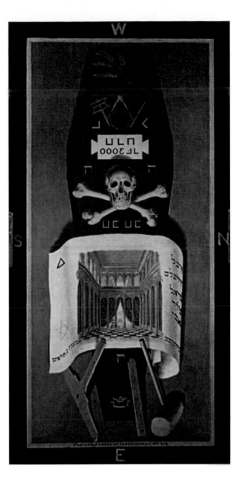

various implements. In the centre, a pedestal supports an Open Book, on which the Square and the Compasses lie. A Ladder reaches upwards to the Blazing Star in the heavens, where the sun, moon, and seven other stars are also depicted. The symbols on the Ladder's rungs represent moral virtues.

The Second Degree Tracing Board shows the interior of King Solomon's Temple, looking towards the inner sanctum. The two pillars represent Jachin and Boaz, the Winding Staircase leading to the Holy of Holies. The River Jordan can be seen in the background with a small waterfall and an ear of growing corn.

The Third Degree Tracing Board has a solid black border. This has a dual meaning – it is a symbol of mourning and a representation of an open grave. The Coffin has an acacia bush near its head, while the interior of King Solomon's Temple is again depicted – this time as a vignette on the Coffin. The emblems of mortality and the Working Tools of a Master Mason and a craftsman are also displayed. Near the head of the Coffin is an inscribed plaque.

ABOVE LEFT The First Degree Tracing Board, includes a Ladder and the three pillars, and describes the place of the human individual in a broad context.

ABOVE MIDDLE The Second Degree Tracing Board shows King Solomon's Temple, in which the individual can ascend a spiral staircase leading to the interior.

ABOVE RIGHT The Third Degree Tracing Board includes a Coffin, which is an analogy of death, whereby the individual will transcend his ordinary life and reach richer things.

LEFT These Viennese Masons in a 1791 illustration are using a Tracing Board as an aid to understanding the symbolism of one of the Degree ceremonies.

GLOSSARY

Acacia
An evergreen shrub which, in Freemasonry, is a symbol of the immortality of the soul.

Age
The time Masons need to serve before they can progress to a higher degree. For an Entered Apprentice, it is three years, for a Fellow Craft Mason five years and for a Master Mason seven years.

Alarm
A signal of someone seeking admission to a lodge. It is given by the Tyler knocking distinctly three times on the door to the lodge room.

Allegiance
A Mason owes allegiance first and foremost to the lodge in which his membership is held and second to the Grand Lodge under which his lodge is chartered. Lodge members swear secret oaths and perform secret rituals swearing allegiance to the lodge and its teachings.

Altar
The centrepiece of the lodge room.

Apron
The "badge of a Mason", the first gift he receives, the first symbol to be explained, and the first tangible evidence of admission into the Craft. It is made from white lambskin, which signifies innocence and the need for purity in life and conduct.

Ark
In Freemasonry, the symbol of the lodge, or a chest containing Masonic Warrants, Jewels and Emblems.

Ashlar
A term used by stonemasons to describe stone as it comes out of a quarry. In the First Degree the Rough Ashlar – the unworked stone – is symbolic of man in his natural state. The Perfect Ashlar symbolizes what he can become through Masonic education.

Beauty
One of the three symbolic supports of the Lodge, represented by the Corinthian column, the Junior Warden, who symbolizes the sun at its meridian, and Hiram Abif, because the beauty and glory of King Solomon's Temple were the result of his skill.

Blue Lodge
The basic Masonic Lodge granting the first Three Degrees. The term "Blue Lodge" has gained more widespread usage in recent times, but "Craft Lodge" is the more usual term in the UK.

Boaz
The name of the left-hand pillar that stood in the porch of King Solomon's Temple.

Book of Constitutions
The rules, regulations and legends of the Craft, compiled by James Anderson and first published in 1723.

Cable Tow
A rope for leading or drawing, which features in the rituals of the Three Degrees.

Cardinal Virtues
Freemasonry has four Cardinal Virtues – Fortitude, Prudence, Temperance and Justice.

Chaos
A symbol of the ignorance and intellectual darkness from which man can be rescued by the light and truth of the Craft.

Clean Hands
An emblem of purity. The white gloves worn during Masonic ceremonies are a direct allusion to the symbol.

Colours
Masonic colours represent the four elements: white symbolizes the earth, purple the sea, sky blue is the air and crimson is fire.

Cornerstone
In Masonic buildings the cornerstone is always placed in the north-east corner. Its surfaces must be square and its solid contents a cube – symbols of morality and truth. Its positioning symbolizes progress from ignorance to knowledge.

Cowan
One of the uninitiated, from who Masonic secrets must be kept.

Darkness to Light
All candidates for the Three Degrees are required to enter the lodge in total darkness as a necessary preliminary to receiving the Light they wish for and seek.

Degree
A grade that prepares a Freemason to go to another higher degree. The first three degrees are Entered Apprentice, Fellow Craft and Master Mason.

East
In Freemasonry the east, where the Master of the Lodge sits, is symbolic of light. Lodge

halls and rooms are oblong from east to west, while candidates for the Three Degrees progress from west to east in search of Light.

Five
Among Masons five is a sacred number, second in importance only to three and seven. In the Fellow Craft Degree, for instance, five men are required to hold a lodge, while in the Third Degree, there are references to five points of fellowship and the symbol of the five-pointed star.

Floor Cloth
A framework of board or canvas on which the emblems of any particular degree are inscribed to aid the Master of the Lodge when lecturing.

G
The symbol for God or Geometry. It is usually painted on the east wall of a lodge or sculpted in wood or metal and hung over the Master's chair.

High Twelve
The Masonic term for noon, when members of a lodge are called to take refreshment from their labours.

Jachin
The name of the right-hand column in the porch of King Solomon's Temple. It is associated with establishment, legality, the Junior Warden and the Fellow Craft.

Jewels
Every Masonic Lodge has six jewels – three Immovable and three Movable. In English Masonry the former are the Square, Level and Plumb Line and the latter the two Ashlars and the Trestle-board. The opposite is the case in American Masonry.

Labyrinth
A symbol of the journey through life.

Landmarks
The most important are the methods of recognition, the government of the Craft and the prerogatives of the Grand Master.

Liberal Arts
The seven arts and sciences decreed worthy of study in Second Degree Freemasonry.

Light
The Lesser Lights are candles placed east, west and south in the lodge, while the Fixed Lights are the windows to the east, west and south. The Three Great Lights are the Volume of Sacred Law, the Square and the Compasses.

Maul
An old name for a mallet.

Oblong Square
A symbol of the lodge, King Solomon's Temple and Noah's Ark.

Pedestals
Substitutes for the three columns of Wisdom, Strength, and Beauty. The three superior officers of the lodge sit at them.

Piece of Architecture
Any work of literature dealing with the Craft.

Serpent
A symbol of wisdom and healing. When depicted with its tail in its mouth, it symbolizes eternity.

So Mote It Be
The Masonic equivalent of Amen.

Tracing Boards
A means of recording the emblems associated with a particular Masonic Degree.

Trestle-board
The board on which the Master of the Lodge draws in a symbolic act representing the building of temples in heart and mind.

Triangle
Equilateral triangles are symbols of perfection; double triangles of deity; and triple triangles, or pentalpha, of health and fellowship.

Tyler
The name of the office of the outer guard of the Freemason's lodge, who guards the door.

Winding Staircase
The way up to the middle chamber of the temple. The steps, spiral and columns have important Masonic significance.

INDEX

A

acacias 47, 83
alchemy 25, 62
All-Seeing Eye 45, 58–9
allegory, importance of 11
American Revolution 27
Ancient Mysteries 18–19
Ancients, the 26–7
Anderson, James 40
Anti-Masonic Party 30
Antient Grand Lodge 62
Apprentice Pillar, Rosslyn
    Chapel 15
Apron, the 88–9
architecture 32–41
    building plans 76–7
    lodges and temples 19, 42–5
Ark of the Covenant 37
Ashmole, Elias 25
astrology 60
astronomy 60, 65
atheists 30

B

Babel, Tower of 76
Bacon, Francis 24
Bannaker, Benjamin 76
beehives 78, 79
bees 78, 79
Belcher, Jonathan 27
Belgium 26
Bible, the 8, 29, 49
Blazing Star 44, 60, 61, 66–7
blue, for decoration 45
Blue Lodge Masonry 28, 43,
    72, 84
Boaz 16, 29, 45, 56–7
Book of Constitutions 73

Book of the Dead 43
book symbols 78
Boston Tea Party 27
Boswell, John, Laird of
    Auchenleck 23
Boyle, Robert 24
Broken Column 78
Brongniart, Alexandre-
    Théodore 47

C

Cagliostro, Count Alessandro
    39
candles 43, 56–7
Canonbury Tower, London 24
Castle Howard, Yorkshire 46
Chartres Cathedral, France
    34–5
chequered floors 45, 66–7
Christianity 9, 15, 26, 78,
    82, 86
    see also Roman Catholic
    Church
Churchill, Winston 31
cities, layouts of 76–7
Clement V, Pope 14
Clement XII, Pope 31
Coffin and Skull, the 70–1
colour 44
columns 56–7
    Broken Column 78
Compasses, the 8–9, 19, 21, 50
Cook Manuscript 17
Corinthian order 40
cornerstones 78
Cornucopia 84
Corpus Hermeticum 22
Cross, Jeremy 78

D

Daedalus 21, 54
Dagger, the 73
Danton, Georges 27
David, King 64
Declaration of Independence
    27
Dee, Dr John 25
Doric order 40
Dreyfus Affair 31

E

Egypt, ancient 18, 20–1,
    38–9, 45, 46, 54–5, 58,
    60, 78, 83
Egyptian Rite 39
Eleusinian Mysteries 21
Ellicott, Andrew 76
Enlightenment, the 26–7, 38
Enoch, legend of 17
Entered Apprentice initiation
    28–9, 62, 73
Euclid 74
Eye of Horus 59
eye symbols 58–9

F

Fellow Craft Mason initiation
    29, 41, 82
Flavius Josephus 52
floor cloths 43
floors
    chequered 45, 66–7
Fortitude 81
Four Cardinal Virtues 80–1
France 26, 27, 30, 31, 46
    Chartres Cathedral 34–5
Franklin, Benjamin 27
Frederick the Great 12
funerary gardens 47

G

Galileo 25
gardens 46–7
Garibaldi, Giuseppe 31
Gauge, the 24-inch 50
Gavel, the 50–1
geometry 16, 25, 74–5
George Washington Masonic
    National Memorial 45

Germany 26, 46
globes 64–5
Goethe, Johann Wolfgang von
    12, 47
Grand Lodge No. 1 Manuscript
    17
Great Lights, the 8
Greeks, Ancient 16, 21, 82

H

Hall, Manly P. 39
Hancock, John 27
handgrips 11
Hawksmoor, Nicholas 47
heather 83
Hermes Trismegistus 38, 47,
    55
Herod the Great, King 52
High Twelve 18
Hiram, King of Tyre 11
Hiram Abif 11, 16, 18, 20, 47,
    71, 78
    rituals 18, 29, 70–1
Hitler, Adolf 31
Holocaust, the 31
Hour Glass, the 80

I

Imhotep 55
Immovable Jewels 84–5
Indented Tassel 61, 67
initiation rituals
    First Degree (Entered
    Apprentice) 28–9,
    62, 73
    Second Degree (Fellow Craft
    Mason) 29, 41, 82
    Third Degree (Master
    Mason) 18, 29, 70–1, 82–3
Innocent II, Pope 14
Invisible College 24–5
Ionic order 40
Italy 26, 31

J

Jachin 16, 29, 45, 56–7
Jackson, Andrew 30
Jacob's Ladder 68–9
James VI and I, King of
    Scotland and England 22–3

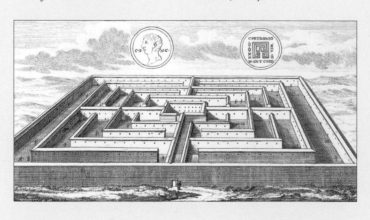

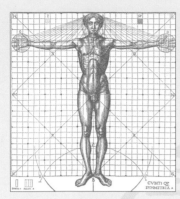

Jefferson, Thomas 76
jewels 84–5

K
Kent, William 47
key symbols 84–5
Kilbourne, Hector 77
King Solomon's Temple 9, 11,
    16, 35, 36–7, 44, 52–3
Knights Templar 10, 14, 15

L
labyrinths 21, 35, 54
ladders 68–9
Lafayette, Marquis de 27
Langley, Batty 40–1
Le Nôtre, André 76
L'Enfant, Pierre Charles 76
Leo XII, Pope 31
Leo XIII, Pope 31
Lesser Lights 63–4
lettuce 83
Level, the 50, 62, 84, 85
lilies 16
lodges (temples) 19, 42–5
lotus 83

M
Mainz, Archbishop of 60
maps 65
Master Mason initiation 18, 29,
    70–1, 82–3
Maurras, Charles 31
mazes *see* labyrinths
Mazzini, Giuseppe 31
Mercury (god) 47
Mesopotamia 18, 86
Minos, King 21
mistletoe 83
Mithraism 19
Molay, Jacques de 14
Moon, the 62–3
Moon Lodges 63

Mosaic Pavement 43, 66–7
Movable Jewels 84, 85
Mozart, Wolfgang Amadeus 12
Mussolini, Benito 31
mystery cults 18–19

N
Napoleon 38
Newton, Isaac 24
noon 18
Norton, Eliot Charles 59

O
obelisks 38, 39, 46
Old Charges 16–17
olive oil 82
Open Book, the 78
Operative Masonry 13, 23, 35
orders of architecture 40
origins 10–11, 14–15
Osiris (god) 16, 18, 20, 44

P
Palladio, Andrea 41
passwords 11
Pennsylvania, Grand Lodge of
    26
pentagrams 21, 86–7
Perdix 21
Père-Lachaise, Paris 47
Perfect Ashlar 32, 62, 85
Philip IV, King of France 14
Pike, Albert 44
pillars 16, 56–7
    see also Boaz; Jachin
Plumb, the 50, 62, 84, 85
plumb line, invention of 21
pomegranates 16
Premier Grand Lodge 26,
    44, 62
Preston, William 65
Prudence 81
Ptah (god) 55
pyramids 38, 39, 46, 47, 54–5
Pythagoras 21, 40, 69, 74

R
Re (god) 60
Reagan, Ronald 31
Regius Manuscript 17
Renaissance 22–3
Roman Catholic Church 9, 22,
    25, 27, 30–1
Rome, Ancient 18, 78

Roosevelt, Franklin Delano 31
Rosslyn Chapel, Scotland 15
rotundas 46
Rough Ashlar 32, 62
Rousseau, Jean-Jacques 46
Royal Arch Degree 28
Royal Arch Halls, Chapter
    Room, Edinburgh 45
Royal Society, London 24, 25
Russia 26

S
St Clair, Sir William 15
Sandusky, Ohio 77
Schaw, Sir William 22
Scotland 14–15, 22–3, 45, 56
Scottish Rite 28, 44
Scythe, the 80
secrecy 11, 22, 25, 43
Sieyès, Emmanuel-Joseph
    27
Silvergate Temple, San Diego
    45
Skull, the 70–1
Solomon, King 9, 11, 18,
    36, 64
    see also King Solomon's
    Temple
Speculative Masonry, origins
    12, 23, 25, 34, 35
sphinxes 38, 39, 46
Square, the 8, 19, 50, 62, 84,
    85
stairs 68–9
star symbols
    Blazing Star 44, 60, 61, 66–7
    five- and seven-pointed 34–5
stonemasons 8–9, 10–11
Stowe, Buckinghamshire
    46, 47
Strawberry Hill, Twickenham
    46
sun, the 60
Switzerland 26
Sword, the 72

T
Temperance 81
temples *see* lodges
Thoth (god) 20
Three Lights, The 28–9
tools *see* Working Tools
Tracing Boards 90–1
Triangle, the 74–5

Trowel, the 51
24-inch Gauge 50
Tyler's Sword 72

U
United Grand Lodge of
    England 27
USA 26, 30, 31
    American Revolution 27
    architecture 42, 76–7
    Great Seal 58–9

V
Vanbrugh, Sir John 47
Vitruvius 40, 41

W
Washington, George 12, 27, 76
    Masonic National Memorial
    45
Washington DC 76–7
wheat 82
Winding Staircase 68
wine 82
women in Masonry 30
Working Tools 50–1
Wren, Christopher 24, 76

Y
York Rite 28, 72

Z
Zodiac, signs of the 44

BIBLIOGRAPHY

The vast number of books on Freemasonry – "the architecture of the craft" as Masons refer to such writings – is daunting. Some are sensational would-be exposés while others are far better. Here are a few of the more thought-provoking. It is also well worth researching the subject on the internet, as many lodges – particularly in the United States – have informative and helpful websites, while some of the classic Masonic texts, which can be hard to find or are out of print, are now available online.

Baignent, Michael, and Leigh, Richard

The Temple and The Lodge (Arcade Publishing, New York, 1989)

Carr, Harry

The Freemason at Work (Lewis Masonic, Shepperton, 1992)

Coil, James Stevens

Coil's Masonic Encyclopaedia (Anchor Communications, Virginia, 1991)

Cotterell, Maurice M.

The Tutankhamun Prophecies (Hodder Headline, London, 1999)

Curl, James Stevens

The Art & Architecture of Freemasonry (Batsford, London, 1991)

Duncan, Malcolm C.

Duncan's Ritual of Freemasonry (Crown, New York, 1976)

Dyer, Colin

Symbolism in Craft Masonry (Ian Allen, Shepperton, 1986)

Hamill, John

The Craft: A History of English Freemasonry (Lewis Masonic, Shepperton, 1994)

Hamill, John, and Gilbert, Robert

Freemasonry – A Celebration of the Craft (Aquarian Press, London, 1991)

Jacob, Margaret E.

Living the Enlightenment: Freemasonry and Politics in Eighteenth-Century Europe (Oxford University Press Inc., New York, 1992)

Knight, Christopher, and Lomax, Robert

The Hiram Key (HarperCollins, London, 1996)

Knight, Stephen

Brotherhood: The Secret World of the Freemasons (Stein & Day, New York, 1984)

Lenhoff, Eugen

The Freemasons (Lewis Masonic, Shepperton, 1994)

Mackenzie, Kenneth

The Royal Masonic Cyclopaedia (Thoth Publications, Loughborough, 1987)

Mackey, Albert

A History of Freemasonry (Gramercy Books, New York, 2005)

MacNulty, W. Kirk

Freemasonry: A Journey Through Ritual and Symbol (Thames & Hudson, London, 1991)

Macoy, Robert

Dictionary of Freemasonry (Gramercy Books, New York, 1990)

Ridley, Jasper

The Freemasons (Constable & Robinson, London, 2002)

Robinson, John

Born in Blood: The Lost Secrets of Freemasonry (Evans, New York, 1987)

Short, Martin

Inside the Brotherhood (HarperCollins, London, 1995)

Stevenson, David

The Origins of Freemasonry (Cambridge University Press, Cambridge, 1998)

Wilmhurst, W. L.

The Meaning of Masonry (Gramercy Books, New York, 1995).

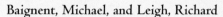